RENEWED

SET IN SOUL

THIS JOURNAL BELONGS TO

_____

DEDICATED TO THOSE MOVING
FORWARD. PROGRESSION.

TABLE OF CONTENTS

HOW TO USE THIS JOURNAL

You can never be better until you get better. It doesn't matter how great everything looks on the outside if in the inside you are not at peace. You know this. You understand this. This is why you now possess this journal titled RENEWED. That is what you want to be: RENEWED. You have acknowledged that now is the time to put to rest whatever it is inside of you that needs healing and to receive a renewal of your thoughts, attitude, and spirit. The Bible says, "Create in me a clean heart, O God, and renew a right spirit within me." —Psalm 51:10. Whether you need help forgiving yourself or another, coming to terms with your past, friends, or family members, or letting go of something you may have wanted, this journal will walk you through the process of healing from the pain that is keeping you from inner peace. This journal is only an aid, and it is recommended that you also seek out other healthy practices of healing if needed. We recommend prayer and positive affirmations to enhance your ability to release pain, a burden that no one should have to carry.

This is the time to be completely honest with yourself. Write it all down. Let your spirit guide you as you see your words on paper. At times, it may be a challenge for you to write past your tears. That's when you take a quick break to release the pain and then get back to writing. This should be a daily practice until you believe that you are able and ready to accept things for what they are and truly heal and move forward in a healthy direction. This journal is divided into four sections with daily writing prompts. Sometimes you might answer the questions the same way you did the day before, and other times you may feel completely different. The best time to reflect in this journal is right before you go to bed. Once you have put to rest what is hurting you, recite positive affirmations about yourself and remember that God has freed you from the pain. Motivational quotes are sprinkled throughout this journal. Feel free to cut them out and post them on the wall for daily inspiration. Get to the bottom of what's really affecting you, and start seeing past your own pain. Be gentle with yourself and be okay with your truth. Replenish your heart with true unconditional love for yourself and be renewed.

QUESTIONS TOWARDS MY HEALING

Who Has Hurt Me In The Past?

mother
Father   younger brother
Son
Boyfriend / Husband
Friend

Who Is Currently Hurting Me?

What Exactly Is Hurting Me?

The Reason It Hurts Me:

What Is The Truth In My Hurt?

QUESTIONS TOWARDS MY HEALING

What Is The Lie In My Hurt?

How Have I Allowed The Hurt To Control Me?

Who Am I Upset At More?

At What Point Will I Realize That The Person Who Has Hurt Me Is Actually More Hurt Than Me?

If Any, What Role Did I Play In Getting Hurt?

QUESTIONS TOWARDS MY HEALING

What Am I Resisting From Entering My Life Because I Am Hurt?

Why Do I Continue To Allow The Hurt To Have An Impact On Me?

Who Is Being Impacted By My Hurt?

I Have Been Dealing With This Hurt For (State How Long):

What I Must Come To Peace With:

QUESTIONS TOWARDS MY HEALING

The Questions I Keep Asking Myself Are:

I Turn Positive Thoughts Into Positive Affirmations By:

I Know The Pain Hurt Me, But It Did Not:

Name The Hurt (Give It A Name):

What Would You Like To Say To (Name)?

QUESTIONS TOWARDS MY HEALING

Although I Wish Things Could Be Different, I Now Know:

What The Hurt Took From Me:

The Things I Have Been Trying To Get From Others That I Can Give To Myself:

The Expectations That I Have Placed On Others That Has Let Me Down Are:

Do I Make Excuses For Myself And/Or Others?

If Yes To The Previous Question, Why Do I Make Excuses For Myself And/ Or Others?

I Have Now Stopped Making Excuses For:

What Scares Me?

I Can Overcome What Scares Me By:

Nobody Knows That I:

QUESTIONS TOWARDS MY HEALING

The Biggest Lie I Have Ever Told Myself:

What I Know About Myself:

I Have Accepted:

The Biggest Thing I've Done That Has Hurt Me:

I Choose To Move Forward By:

QUESTIONS TOWARDS MY HEALING

I Will Avoid:

I Will No Longer Accept:

I Am:

I Am Open To:

I Believe:

QUESTIONS TOWARDS MY HEALING

The Most Important Thing Right Now Is:

I Am Choosing To Focus On:

I Am Choosing To Overcome:

What I Like About Myself:

What Makes Me Feel Safe:

QUESTIONS TOWARDS MY HEALING

When I Am Hurt And/Or Sad, I Turn To:

The Healthiest Way For Me To Heal Is:

In My Healing, I Will Not Be Distracted By:

I Love The Way I Handle:

I Am Deciding:

QUESTIONS TOWARDS MY HEALING

I Deserve:

It Is Time For Me To:

Right Now, It Means A Lot To Me That:

I Would Like To Be Protected From:

Moving Forward, The Best Way To Protect Myself Without Blocking My Future Opportunities Are:

Section One:

BECAUSE OF THEM. BECAUSE OF ME.

BECAUSE OF THEM. BECAUSE OF ME.

Date: _____

Mood: _____

I Need More:

When I Think Of_____

_____, I Think

My Spirit Tells Me:

I Feel Most Like Myself When:

I Am Choosing To Believe _____

_____ About

When I Think Of (Name The Person),

_____I Feel:

I Am Grateful That_____

_____

This Person Makes Me Feel This Way
Because:

Happened, Because Now I Can

What This Person Took From Me:

I Need To Forgive_____

_____Because

Because Of Their Actions/What They
Said, I:

I Kept Wondering Why _____

_____,

But Now I

I Will No Longer Give Them The Power
To:

I Can Heal From_____

_____ Because I

I Am Taking Control Of How I Feel By:

BECAUSE OF THEM. BECAUSE OF ME.

Date: Mood:

I Need More:

My Spirit Tells Me:

I Feel Most Like Myself When:

When I Think Of (Name The Person),

_____I Feel:

This Person Makes Me Feel This Way
Because:

What This Person Took From Me:

Because Of Their Actions/What They
Said, I:

I Will No Longer Give Them The Power
To:

I Am Taking Control Of How I Feel By:

When I Think Of_____

_____, I Think

I Am Choosing To Believe _____

_____ About

I Am Grateful That_____

_____

Happened, Because Now I Can

I Need To Forgive_____

_____Because

I Kept Wondering Why _____

_____,

But Now I

I Can Heal From_____

_____ Because I

21

IT DOESN'T MATTER HOW I AM PERCEIVED. I KNOW WHO I AM.

BECAUSE OF THEM. BECAUSE OF ME.

Date: Mood:

I Need More: When I Think Of_____

_____, I Think

My Spirit Tells Me:

I Feel Most Like Myself When: I Am Choosing To Believe _____

_____ About

When I Think Of (Name The Person),

_____I Feel: I Am Grateful That_____

_____

This Person Makes Me Feel This Way   Happened, Because Now I Can
Because:

I Need To Forgive_____

What This Person Took From Me: _____Because

Because Of Their Actions/What They   I Kept Wondering Why _____
Said, I:
_____,

But Now I

I Will No Longer Give Them The Power
To: I Can Heal From_____

_____ Because I

I Am Taking Control Of How I Feel By:

BECAUSE OF THEM. BECAUSE OF ME.

Date:

Mood:

I Need More:

When I Think Of_____

_____, I Think

My Spirit Tells Me:

I Feel Most Like Myself When:

I Am Choosing To Believe _____

_____ About

When I Think Of (Name The Person),

_____I Feel:

I Am Grateful That_____

_____

This Person Makes Me Feel This Way
Because:

Happened, Because Now I Can

What This Person Took From Me:

I Need To Forgive_____

_____Because

Because Of Their Actions/What They
Said, I:

I Kept Wondering Why _____

_____,

But Now I

I Will No Longer Give Them The Power
To:

I Can Heal From_____

_____ Because I

I Am Taking Control Of How I Feel By:

24

BECAUSE OF THEM. BECAUSE OF ME.

Date:

Mood:

I Need More:

When I Think Of_____

_____, I Think

My Spirit Tells Me:

I Feel Most Like Myself When:

I Am Choosing To Believe _____

_____ About

When I Think Of (Name The Person),

_____I Feel:

I Am Grateful That_____

_____

This Person Makes Me Feel This Way Because:

Happened, Because Now I Can

What This Person Took From Me:

I Need To Forgive_____

_____Because

Because Of Their Actions/What They Said, I:

I Kept Wondering Why _____

_____,

But Now I

I Will No Longer Give Them The Power To:

I Can Heal From_____

_____ Because I

I Am Taking Control Of How I Feel By:

THEY ARE STILL THE OLD THEM, THAT IS WHY THEY KEEP BRINGING UP THE OLD ME.

I WILL BE JUDGED, CRITICIZED AND RIDICULED. I WILL BE TALKED ABOUT. I WILL FORGIVE IT ALL.

BECAUSE OF THEM. BECAUSE OF ME.

Date:

Mood:

I Need More:

When I Think Of_____

_____, I Think

My Spirit Tells Me:

I Feel Most Like Myself When:

I Am Choosing To Believe _____

_____ About

When I Think Of (Name The Person),

_____I Feel:

I Am Grateful That_____

_____

This Person Makes Me Feel This Way
Because:

Happened, Because Now I Can

What This Person Took From Me:

I Need To Forgive_____

_____Because

Because Of Their Actions/What They
Said, I:

I Kept Wondering Why _____

_____,

But Now I

I Will No Longer Give Them The Power
To:

I Can Heal From_____

_____ Because I

I Am Taking Control Of How I Feel By:

BECAUSE OF THEM. BECAUSE OF ME.

Date: Mood:

I Need More: When I Think Of_____

                                         _____, I Think

My Spirit Tells Me:

I Feel Most Like Myself When: I Am Choosing To Believe _____

                                         _____ About

When I Think Of (Name The Person),

_____I Feel: I Am Grateful That_____

                                         _____

This Person Makes Me Feel This Way   Happened, Because Now I Can
Because:

                                         I Need To Forgive_____

What This Person Took From Me: _____Because

Because Of Their Actions/What They
Said, I: I Kept Wondering Why _____

                                         _____,

                                         But Now I

I Will No Longer Give Them The Power
To: I Can Heal From_____

                                         _____ Because I

I Am Taking Control Of How I Feel By:

BECAUSE OF THEM. BECAUSE OF ME.

Date:

Mood:

I Need More:

When I Think Of_____

_____, I Think

My Spirit Tells Me:

I Feel Most Like Myself When:

I Am Choosing To Believe _____

_____ About

When I Think Of (Name The Person),

_____I Feel:

I Am Grateful That_____

_____

This Person Makes Me Feel This Way
Because:

Happened, Because Now I Can

What This Person Took From Me:

I Need To Forgive_____

_____Because

Because Of Their Actions/What They
Said, I:

I Kept Wondering Why _____

_____,

But Now I

I Will No Longer Give Them The Power
To:

I Can Heal From_____

_____ Because I

I Am Taking Control Of How I Feel By:

BECAUSE OF THEM. BECAUSE OF ME.

Date:

Mood:

I Need More:

When I Think Of_____

_____, I Think

My Spirit Tells Me:

I Feel Most Like Myself When:

I Am Choosing To Believe _____

_____ About

When I Think Of (Name The Person),

_____I Feel:

I Am Grateful That_____

_____

This Person Makes Me Feel This Way
Because:

Happened, Because Now I Can

What This Person Took From Me:

I Need To Forgive_____

_____Because

Because Of Their Actions/What They
Said, I:

I Kept Wondering Why _____

_____,

But Now I

I Will No Longer Give Them The Power
To:

I Can Heal From_____

_____ Because I

I Am Taking Control Of How I Feel By:

BECAUSE OF THEM. BECAUSE OF ME.

Date:

Mood:

I Need More:

When I Think Of_____

_____, I Think

My Spirit Tells Me:

I Feel Most Like Myself When:

I Am Choosing To Believe _____

_____ About

When I Think Of (Name The Person),

_____I Feel:

I Am Grateful That_____

_____

This Person Makes Me Feel This Way Because:

Happened, Because Now I Can

What This Person Took From Me:

I Need To Forgive_____

_____Because

Because Of Their Actions/What They Said, I:

I Kept Wondering Why _____

_____,

But Now I

I Will No Longer Give Them The Power To:

I Can Heal From_____

_____ Because I

I Am Taking Control Of How I Feel By:

INSECURITIES I HAVE THAT ARE HINDERING ME ARE....

BECAUSE OF THEM. BECAUSE OF ME.

Date:

Mood:

I Need More:

When I Think Of_____

_____, I Think

My Spirit Tells Me:

I Feel Most Like Myself When:

I Am Choosing To Believe _____

_____ About

When I Think Of (Name The Person),

_____I Feel:

I Am Grateful That_____

_____

This Person Makes Me Feel This Way
Because:

Happened, Because Now I Can

What This Person Took From Me:

I Need To Forgive_____

_____Because

Because Of Their Actions/What They
Said, I:

I Kept Wondering Why _____

_____,

But Now I

I Will No Longer Give Them The Power
To:

I Can Heal From_____

_____ Because I

I Am Taking Control Of How I Feel By:

BECAUSE OF THEM. BECAUSE OF ME.

Date: Mood:

I Need More: When I Think Of_____

_____, I Think

My Spirit Tells Me:

I Feel Most Like Myself When: I Am Choosing To Believe _____

_____ About

When I Think Of (Name The Person),

_____I Feel: I Am Grateful That_____

_____

This Person Makes Me Feel This Way Happened, Because Now I Can
Because:

I Need To Forgive_____

What This Person Took From Me: _____Because

Because Of Their Actions/What They
Said, I: I Kept Wondering Why _____

_____,

But Now I

I Will No Longer Give Them The Power
To: I Can Heal From_____

_____ Because I

I Am Taking Control Of How I Feel By:

35

I HAVE STOPPED SAYING YES TO WHAT DESERVES A NO.

THE REASON I GET EASILY FRUSTRATED....

BECAUSE OF THEM. BECAUSE OF ME.

Date:

Mood:

I Need More:

When I Think Of_____

_____, I Think

My Spirit Tells Me:

I Feel Most Like Myself When:

I Am Choosing To Believe _____

_____ About

When I Think Of (Name The Person),

_____I Feel:

I Am Grateful That_____

_____

This Person Makes Me Feel This Way
Because:

Happened, Because Now I Can

What This Person Took From Me:

I Need To Forgive_____

_____Because

Because Of Their Actions/What They
Said, I:

I Kept Wondering Why _____

_____,

But Now I

I Will No Longer Give Them The Power
To:

I Can Heal From_____

_____ Because I

I Am Taking Control Of How I Feel By:

BECAUSE OF THEM. BECAUSE OF ME.

Date: _____   Mood: _____

I Need More:

When I Think Of_____

_____, I Think

My Spirit Tells Me:

I Feel Most Like Myself When:

I Am Choosing To Believe _____

_____ About

When I Think Of (Name The Person),

_____I Feel:

I Am Grateful That_____

_____

This Person Makes Me Feel This Way
Because:

Happened, Because Now I Can

What This Person Took From Me:

I Need To Forgive_____

_____Because

Because Of Their Actions/What They
Said, I:

I Kept Wondering Why _____

_____,

But Now I

I Will No Longer Give Them The Power
To:

I Can Heal From_____

_____ Because I

I Am Taking Control Of How I Feel By:

THERE WILL BE PEOPLE WHO PLOTTED AGAINST ME AND WONDERED HOW I SURVIVED. THEY DON'T KNOW ABOUT GOD'S GRACE IN MY LIFE.

BECAUSE OF THEM. BECAUSE OF ME.

Date:

Mood:

I Need More:

When I Think Of_____

_____, I Think

My Spirit Tells Me:

I Feel Most Like Myself When:

I Am Choosing To Believe _____

_____ About

When I Think Of (Name The Person),

_____I Feel:

I Am Grateful That_____

_____

This Person Makes Me Feel This Way
Because:

Happened, Because Now I Can

What This Person Took From Me:

I Need To Forgive_____

_____Because

Because Of Their Actions/What They
Said, I:

I Kept Wondering Why _____

_____,

But Now I

I Will No Longer Give Them The Power
To:

I Can Heal From_____

_____ Because I

I Am Taking Control Of How I Feel By:

BECAUSE OF THEM. BECAUSE OF ME.

Date:

Mood:

I Need More:

When I Think Of_____

_____, I Think

My Spirit Tells Me:

I Feel Most Like Myself When:

I Am Choosing To Believe _____

_____ About

When I Think Of (Name The Person),

_____I Feel:

I Am Grateful That_____

_____

This Person Makes Me Feel This Way Because:

Happened, Because Now I Can

What This Person Took From Me:

I Need To Forgive_____

_____Because

Because Of Their Actions/What They Said, I:

I Kept Wondering Why _____

_____,

But Now I

I Will No Longer Give Them The Power To:

I Can Heal From_____

_____ Because I

I Am Taking Control Of How I Feel By:

I HAVE LET GO OF MY FEAR OF BEING REJECTED BY ....

BECAUSE OF THEM. BECAUSE OF ME.

Date:

Mood:

I Need More:

When I Think Of_____

_____, I Think

My Spirit Tells Me:

I Feel Most Like Myself When:

I Am Choosing To Believe _____

_____ About

When I Think Of (Name The Person),

_____I Feel:

I Am Grateful That_____

_____

This Person Makes Me Feel This Way Because:

Happened, Because Now I Can

I Need To Forgive_____

What This Person Took From Me:

_____Because

Because Of Their Actions/What They Said, I:

I Kept Wondering Why _____

_____,

But Now I

I Will No Longer Give Them The Power To:

I Can Heal From_____

_____ Because I

I Am Taking Control Of How I Feel By:

BECAUSE OF THEM. BECAUSE OF ME.

Date: Mood:

I Need More: When I Think Of_____

_____, I Think

My Spirit Tells Me:

I Feel Most Like Myself When: I Am Choosing To Believe _____

_____ About

When I Think Of (Name The Person),

_____I Feel: I Am Grateful That_____

_____

This Person Makes Me Feel This Way   Happened, Because Now I Can
Because:

What This Person Took From Me: I Need To Forgive_____

_____Because

Because Of Their Actions/What They   I Kept Wondering Why _____
Said, I:

_____,

But Now I

I Will No Longer Give Them The Power   I Can Heal From_____
To:

_____ Because I

I Am Taking Control Of How I Feel By:

45

BECAUSE OF THEM. BECAUSE OF ME.

Date:

Mood:

I Need More:

When I Think Of_____

_____, I Think

My Spirit Tells Me:

I Feel Most Like Myself When:

I Am Choosing To Believe _____

_____ About

When I Think Of (Name The Person),

_____I Feel:

I Am Grateful That_____

_____

This Person Makes Me Feel This Way
Because:

Happened, Because Now I Can

What This Person Took From Me:

I Need To Forgive_____

_____Because

Because Of Their Actions/What They
Said, I:

I Kept Wondering Why _____

_____,

But Now I

I Will No Longer Give Them The Power
To:

I Can Heal From_____

_____ Because I

I Am Taking Control Of How I Feel By:

FOR A LONG TIME I HAVE AVOIDED ....

MY HURT WAS HEALED BY PRAYER.
MY HURT WAS HEALED BECAUSE I SURRENDERED.
MY HURT WAS HEALED BECAUSE I FORGAVE.

BECAUSE OF THEM. BECAUSE OF ME.

Date: Mood:

I Need More: When I Think Of_____

_____, I Think

My Spirit Tells Me:

I Feel Most Like Myself When: I Am Choosing To Believe _____

_____ About

When I Think Of (Name The Person),

_____I Feel: I Am Grateful That_____

_____

This Person Makes Me Feel This Way   Happened, Because Now I Can
Because:

I Need To Forgive_____

What This Person Took From Me: _____Because

Because Of Their Actions/What They
Said, I: I Kept Wondering Why _____

_____,

But Now I

I Will No Longer Give Them The Power
To: I Can Heal From_____

_____ Because I

I Am Taking Control Of How I Feel By:

BECAUSE OF THEM. BECAUSE OF ME.

Date: Mood:

I Need More: When I Think Of_____

_____, I Think

My Spirit Tells Me:

I Feel Most Like Myself When: I Am Choosing To Believe _____

_____ About

When I Think Of (Name The Person),

_____I Feel: I Am Grateful That_____

_____

This Person Makes Me Feel This Way   Happened, Because Now I Can
Because:

What This Person Took From Me: I Need To Forgive_____

_____Because

Because Of Their Actions/What They
Said, I: I Kept Wondering Why _____

_____,

But Now I

I Will No Longer Give Them The Power
To:

I Can Heal From_____

_____ Because I

I Am Taking Control Of How I Feel By:

50

BECAUSE OF THEM. BECAUSE OF ME.

Date:

Mood:

I Need More:

When I Think Of_____

_____, I Think

My Spirit Tells Me:

I Feel Most Like Myself When:

I Am Choosing To Believe _____

_____ About

When I Think Of (Name The Person),

_____I Feel:

I Am Grateful That_____

_____

This Person Makes Me Feel This Way
Because:

Happened, Because Now I Can

What This Person Took From Me:

I Need To Forgive_____

_____Because

Because Of Their Actions/What They
Said, I:

I Kept Wondering Why _____

_____,

But Now I

I Will No Longer Give Them The Power
To:

I Can Heal From_____

_____ Because I

I Am Taking Control Of How I Feel By:

51

IT HAS BEEN HARD FOR ME TO FORGIVE ....

BECAUSE OF THEM. BECAUSE OF ME.

Date:

Mood:

I Need More:

When I Think Of_____

_____, I Think

My Spirit Tells Me:

I Feel Most Like Myself When:

I Am Choosing To Believe _____

_____ About

When I Think Of (Name The Person),

_____I Feel:

I Am Grateful That_____

_____

This Person Makes Me Feel This Way
Because:

Happened, Because Now I Can

What This Person Took From Me:

I Need To Forgive_____

_____Because

Because Of Their Actions/What They
Said, I:

I Kept Wondering Why _____

_____,

But Now I

I Will No Longer Give Them The Power
To:

I Can Heal From_____

_____ Because I

I Am Taking Control Of How I Feel By:

Date: _____   Mood: _____

I Need More:

When I Think Of_____

_____, I Think

My Spirit Tells Me:

I Feel Most Like Myself When:

I Am Choosing To Believe _____

_____ About

When I Think Of (Name The Person),

_____I Feel:

I Am Grateful That_____

_____

This Person Makes Me Feel This Way
Because:

Happened, Because Now I Can

What This Person Took From Me:

I Need To Forgive_____

_____Because

Because Of Their Actions/What They
Said, I:

I Kept Wondering Why _____

_____,

But Now I

I Will No Longer Give Them The Power
To:

I Can Heal From_____

_____ Because I

I Am Taking Control Of How I Feel By:

BECAUSE OF THEM. BECAUSE OF ME.

Date: Mood:

I Need More:

When I Think Of_____

_____, I Think

My Spirit Tells Me:

I Feel Most Like Myself When:

I Am Choosing To Believe _____

_____ About

When I Think Of (Name The Person),

_____I Feel:

I Am Grateful That_____

_____

This Person Makes Me Feel This Way Because:

Happened, Because Now I Can

I Need To Forgive_____

What This Person Took From Me:

_____Because

Because Of Their Actions/What They Said, I:

I Kept Wondering Why _____

_____,

But Now I

I Will No Longer Give Them The Power To:

I Can Heal From_____

_____ Because I

I Am Taking Control Of How I Feel By:

BECAUSE OF THEM. BECAUSE OF ME.

Date:

Mood:

I Need More:

When I Think Of_____

_____, I Think

My Spirit Tells Me:

I Feel Most Like Myself When:

I Am Choosing To Believe _____

_____ About

When I Think Of (Name The Person),

_____I Feel:

I Am Grateful That_____

_____

This Person Makes Me Feel This Way
Because:

Happened, Because Now I Can

What This Person Took From Me:

I Need To Forgive_____

_____Because

Because Of Their Actions/What They
Said, I:

I Kept Wondering Why _____

_____,

But Now I

I Will No Longer Give Them The Power
To:

I Can Heal From_____

_____ Because I

I Am Taking Control Of How I Feel By:

56

BECAUSE OF BUILT UP ANGER, I HAVE ....

BECAUSE OF THEM. BECAUSE OF ME.

Date:

Mood:

I Need More:

When I Think Of_____

_____, I Think

My Spirit Tells Me:

I Feel Most Like Myself When:

I Am Choosing To Believe _____

_____ About

When I Think Of (Name The Person),

_____I Feel:

I Am Grateful That_____

_____

This Person Makes Me Feel This Way
Because:

Happened, Because Now I Can

What This Person Took From Me:

I Need To Forgive_____

_____Because

Because Of Their Actions/What They
Said, I:

I Kept Wondering Why _____

_____,

But Now I

I Will No Longer Give Them The Power
To:

I Can Heal From_____

_____ Because I

I Am Taking Control Of How I Feel By:

I STARTED FIGHTING
FOR ME.

BECAUSE OF THEM. BECAUSE OF ME.

Date: Mood:

I Need More: When I Think Of_____

_____, I Think

My Spirit Tells Me:

I Feel Most Like Myself When: I Am Choosing To Believe _____

_____ About

When I Think Of (Name The Person),

_____I Feel: I Am Grateful That_____

_____

This Person Makes Me Feel This Way   Happened, Because Now I Can
Because:

I Need To Forgive_____

What This Person Took From Me: _____Because

Because Of Their Actions/What They
Said, I: I Kept Wondering Why _____

_____,

But Now I

I Will No Longer Give Them The Power
To:

I Can Heal From_____

I Am Taking Control Of How I Feel By: _____ Because I

60

Date: Mood:

I Need More: When I Think Of_____

_____, I Think

My Spirit Tells Me:

I Feel Most Like Myself When: I Am Choosing To Believe _____

_____ About

When I Think Of (Name The Person),

_____I Feel: I Am Grateful That_____

_____

This Person Makes Me Feel This Way   Happened, Because Now I Can
Because:

I Need To Forgive_____

What This Person Took From Me: _____Because

Because Of Their Actions/What They
Said, I: I Kept Wondering Why _____

_____,

But Now I

I Will No Longer Give Them The Power
To:

I Can Heal From_____

_____ Because I

I Am Taking Control Of How I Feel By:

BECAUSE OF THEM. BECAUSE OF ME.

Date: Mood:

I Need More: When I Think Of_____

_____, I Think

My Spirit Tells Me:

I Feel Most Like Myself When: I Am Choosing To Believe _____

_____ About

When I Think Of (Name The Person),

_____I Feel: I Am Grateful That_____

_____

This Person Makes Me Feel This Way   Happened, Because Now I Can
Because:

I Need To Forgive_____

What This Person Took From Me: _____Because

Because Of Their Actions/What They
Said, I: I Kept Wondering Why _____

_____,

But Now I

I Will No Longer Give Them The Power
To: I Can Heal From_____

_____ Because I

I Am Taking Control Of How I Feel By:

THE THINGS I HAVE DONE BECAUSE I WAS HURT THAT I DEEPLY REGRET....

I HAVE NO DESIRE TO FIT IN. NONE.

BECAUSE OF THEM. BECAUSE OF ME.

Date:

Mood:

I Need More:

When I Think Of_____

_____, I Think

My Spirit Tells Me:

I Feel Most Like Myself When:

I Am Choosing To Believe _____

_____ About

When I Think Of (Name The Person),

_____I Feel:

I Am Grateful That_____

_____

This Person Makes Me Feel This Way
Because:

Happened, Because Now I Can

I Need To Forgive_____

What This Person Took From Me:

_____Because

Because Of Their Actions/What They
Said, I:

I Kept Wondering Why _____

_____,

But Now I

I Will No Longer Give Them The Power
To:

I Can Heal From_____

I Am Taking Control Of How I Feel By:

_____ Because I

BECAUSE OF THEM. BECAUSE OF ME.

Date: Mood:

I Need More: When I Think Of_____

                                         _____, I Think

My Spirit Tells Me:

I Feel Most Like Myself When: I Am Choosing To Believe _____

                                         _____ About

When I Think Of (Name The Person),

_____I Feel: I Am Grateful That_____

                                         _____

This Person Makes Me Feel This Way   Happened, Because Now I Can
Because:

                                         I Need To Forgive_____

What This Person Took From Me: _____Because

Because Of Their Actions/What They   I Kept Wondering Why _____
Said, I:
                                         _____,

                                         But Now I

I Will No Longer Give Them The Power
To:

                                         I Can Heal From_____

I Am Taking Control Of How I Feel By: _____ Because I

Section Two:

BACK THEN

Date:

Mood:

I Am Holding In:

What I Am Expecting To Stop This Hurt Is:

I Thought:

What Was Said That I Have Always Remembered Was:

What Actually Happened:

Back Then, What Was Done/Said Made Me Feel:

I Accepted A Certain Type Of Behavior In The Past Because:

I Hold Grudges Towards:

I Am Still Hurt By (Name The Person And/Or Behavior)

What I Wish I Could Have Done Differently:

_____

Because:

What I Lost Within Me:

I Am Choosing To Let Go Of:

Continue To The Next Page

I Forgive Myself For:

Now I Am Here For Myself By:

I Am Dealing With This Past Situation By:

I Forgive The Hurt And Where The Hurt Came From Because:

I Am Gentle With Myself With:

In Retrospect, I Am Doing Better Now Because:

In The Spirit Of Compassion, I Understand:

What Has Changed Now?

I Show Myself Kindness By:

In The Future, If A Similar Situation Was To Occur, I Will Handle It Better By:

I Applaud Myself For:

Date:

Mood:

I Am Holding In:

What I Am Expecting To Stop This Hurt Is:

I Thought:

What Was Said That I Have Always Remembered Was:

What Actually Happened:

Back Then, What Was Done/Said Made Me Feel:

I Accepted A Certain Type Of Behavior In The Past Because:

I Hold Grudges Towards:

I Am Still Hurt By (Name The Person And/Or Behavior)

What I Wish I Could Have Done Differently:

_____

Because:

What I Lost Within Me:

I Am Choosing To Let Go Of:

Continue To The Next Page

I Forgive Myself For:

Now I Am Here For Myself By:

I Am Dealing With This Past Situation By:

I Forgive The Hurt And Where The Hurt Came From Because:

I Am Gentle With Myself With:

In Retrospect, I Am Doing Better Now Because:

In The Spirit Of Compassion, I Understand:

What Has Changed Now?

I Show Myself Kindness By:

In The Future, If A Similar Situation Was To Occur, I Will Handle It Better By:

I Applaud Myself For:

I NO LONGER BLAME WHO HURT ME BECAUSE ....

HOW PEOPLE TREAT ME WILL NOT DICTATE HOW I TREAT OTHERS.

Date:

Mood:

I Am Holding In:

What I Am Expecting To Stop This Hurt Is:

I Thought:

What Was Said That I Have Always Remembered Was:

What Actually Happened:

Back Then, What Was Done/Said Made Me Feel:

I Accepted A Certain Type Of Behavior In The Past Because:

I Hold Grudges Towards:

I Am Still Hurt By (Name The Person And/Or Behavior)

What I Wish I Could Have Done Differently:

_____

Because:

What I Lost Within Me:

I Am Choosing To Let Go Of:

Continue To The Next Page

I Forgive Myself For:

Now I Am Here For Myself By:

I Am Dealing With This Past Situation By:

I Forgive The Hurt And Where The Hurt Came From Because:

I Am Gentle With Myself With:

In Retrospect, I Am Doing Better Now Because:

In The Spirit Of Compassion, I Understand:

What Has Changed Now?

I Show Myself Kindness By:

In The Future, If A Similar Situation Was To Occur, I Will Handle It Better By:

I Applaud Myself For:

Date: Mood:

I Am Holding In: What I Am Expecting To Stop This Hurt Is:

I Thought: What Was Said That I Have Always
                                          Remembered Was:

What Actually Happened: Back Then, What Was Done/Said Made
                                          Me Feel:

I Accepted A Certain Type Of Behavior   I Hold Grudges Towards:
In The Past Because:

I Am Still Hurt By (Name The   What I Wish I Could Have Done
Person And/Or Behavior)   Differently:

_____

Because:

What I Lost Within Me: I Am Choosing To Let Go Of:

Continue To The Next Page

I Forgive Myself For:

Now I Am Here For Myself By:

I Am Dealing With This Past Situation By:

I Forgive The Hurt And Where The Hurt Came From Because:

I Am Gentle With Myself With:

In Retrospect, I Am Doing Better Now Because:

In The Spirit Of Compassion, I Understand:

What Has Changed Now?

I Show Myself Kindness By:

In The Future, If A Similar Situation Was To Occur, I Will Handle It Better By:

I Applaud Myself For:

Date:

Mood:

I Am Holding In:

What I Am Expecting To Stop This Hurt Is:

I Thought:

What Was Said That I Have Always Remembered Was:

What Actually Happened:

Back Then, What Was Done/Said Made Me Feel:

I Accepted A Certain Type Of Behavior In The Past Because:

I Hold Grudges Towards:

I Am Still Hurt By (Name The Person And/Or Behavior)

What I Wish I Could Have Done Differently:

_____

Because:

What I Lost Within Me:

I Am Choosing To Let Go Of:

Continue To The Next Page

I Forgive Myself For:

Now I Am Here For Myself By:

I Am Dealing With This Past Situation By:

I Forgive The Hurt And Where The Hurt Came From Because:

I Am Gentle With Myself With:

In Retrospect, I Am Doing Better Now Because:

In The Spirit Of Compassion, I Understand:

What Has Changed Now?

I Show Myself Kindness By:

In The Future, If A Similar Situation Was To Occur, I Will Handle It Better By:

I Applaud Myself For:

I FELT HOPELESS
WHEN....

Date:

Mood:

I Am Holding In:

What I Am Expecting To Stop This Hurt Is:

I Thought:

What Was Said That I Have Always Remembered Was:

What Actually Happened:

Back Then, What Was Done/Said Made Me Feel:

I Accepted A Certain Type Of Behavior In The Past Because:

I Hold Grudges Towards:

I Am Still Hurt By (Name The Person And/Or Behavior)

What I Wish I Could Have Done Differently:

_____

Because:

What I Lost Within Me:

I Am Choosing To Let Go Of:

Continue To The Next Page

I Forgive Myself For:

Now I Am Here For Myself By:

I Am Dealing With This Past Situation By:

I Forgive The Hurt And Where The Hurt Came From Because:

I Am Gentle With Myself With:

In Retrospect, I Am Doing Better Now Because:

In The Spirit Of Compassion, I Understand:

What Has Changed Now?

I Show Myself Kindness By:

In The Future, If A Similar Situation Was To Occur, I Will Handle It Better By:

I Applaud Myself For:

Date: Mood:

I Am Holding In: What I Am Expecting To Stop This Hurt Is:

I Thought: What Was Said That I Have Always
                                               Remembered Was:

What Actually Happened: Back Then, What Was Done/Said Made
                                               Me Feel:

I Accepted A Certain Type Of Behavior   I Hold Grudges Towards:
In The Past Because:

I Am Still Hurt By (Name The   What I Wish I Could Have Done
Person And/Or Behavior)   Differently:

_____

Because:

What I Lost Within Me: I Am Choosing To Let Go Of:

Continue To The Next Page

I Forgive Myself For:

Now I Am Here For Myself By:

I Am Dealing With This Past Situation By:

I Forgive The Hurt And Where The Hurt Came From Because:

I Am Gentle With Myself With:

In Retrospect, I Am Doing Better Now Because:

In The Spirit Of Compassion, I Understand:

What Has Changed Now?

I Show Myself Kindness By:

In The Future, If A Similar Situation Was To Occur, I Will Handle It Better By:

I Applaud Myself For:

BACK THEN

Date: Mood:

I Am Holding In: What I Am Expecting To Stop This Hurt Is:

I Thought: What Was Said That I Have Always
                                         Remembered Was:

What Actually Happened: Back Then, What Was Done/Said Made
                                         Me Feel:

I Accepted A Certain Type Of Behavior   I Hold Grudges Towards:
In The Past Because:

I Am Still Hurt By (Name The   What I Wish I Could Have Done
Person And/Or Behavior)   Differently:

_____

Because:

What I Lost Within Me: I Am Choosing To Let Go Of:

Continue To The Next Page

I Forgive Myself For:

Now I Am Here For Myself By:

I Am Dealing With This Past Situation By:

I Forgive The Hurt And Where The Hurt Came From Because:

I Am Gentle With Myself With:

In Retrospect, I Am Doing Better Now Because:

In The Spirit Of Compassion, I Understand:

What Has Changed Now?

I Show Myself Kindness By:

In The Future, If A Similar Situation Was To Occur, I Will Handle It Better By:

I Applaud Myself For:

BACK THEN

Date: Mood:

I Am Holding In: What I Am Expecting To Stop This Hurt Is:

I Thought: What Was Said That I Have Always
                                         Remembered Was:

What Actually Happened: Back Then, What Was Done/Said Made
                                         Me Feel:

I Accepted A Certain Type Of Behavior   I Hold Grudges Towards:
In The Past Because:

I Am Still Hurt By (Name The   What I Wish I Could Have Done
Person And/Or Behavior)   Differently:

_____

Because:

What I Lost Within Me: I Am Choosing To Let Go Of:

Continue To The Next Page

I Forgive Myself For:

Now I Am Here For Myself By:

I Am Dealing With This Past Situation By:

I Forgive The Hurt And Where The Hurt Came From Because:

I Am Gentle With Myself With:

In Retrospect, I Am Doing Better Now Because:

In The Spirit Of Compassion, I Understand:

What Has Changed Now?

I Show Myself Kindness By:

In The Future, If A Similar Situation Was To Occur, I Will Handle It Better By:

I Applaud Myself For:

NO LONGER DO I FEAR MY PAST.

I AM TAKING MY PAIN AND TURNING IT INTO A BLESSING BY....

Date: Mood:

I Am Holding In: What I Am Expecting To Stop This Hurt Is:

I Thought: What Was Said That I Have Always
                                     Remembered Was:

What Actually Happened: Back Then, What Was Done/Said Made
                                     Me Feel:

I Accepted A Certain Type Of Behavior   I Hold Grudges Towards:
In The Past Because:

I Am Still Hurt By (Name The   What I Wish I Could Have Done
Person And/Or Behavior)   Differently:

_____

Because:

What I Lost Within Me: I Am Choosing To Let Go Of:

Continue To The Next Page

I Forgive Myself For:

Now I Am Here For Myself By:

I Am Dealing With This Past Situation By:

I Forgive The Hurt And Where The Hurt Came From Because:

I Am Gentle With Myself With:

In Retrospect, I Am Doing Better Now Because:

In The Spirit Of Compassion, I Understand:

What Has Changed Now?

I Show Myself Kindness By:

In The Future, If A Similar Situation Was To Occur, I Will Handle It Better By:

I Applaud Myself For:

Date: Mood:

I Am Holding In: What I Am Expecting To Stop This Hurt Is:

I Thought: What Was Said That I Have Always
                                         Remembered Was:

What Actually Happened: Back Then, What Was Done/Said Made
                                         Me Feel:

I Accepted A Certain Type Of Behavior   I Hold Grudges Towards:
In The Past Because:

I Am Still Hurt By (Name The   What I Wish I Could Have Done
Person And/Or Behavior)   Differently:

_____

Because:

What I Lost Within Me: I Am Choosing To Let Go Of:

Continue To The Next Page

I Forgive Myself For:

Now I Am Here For Myself By:

I Am Dealing With This Past Situation By:

I Forgive The Hurt And Where The Hurt Came From Because:

I Am Gentle With Myself With:

In Retrospect, I Am Doing Better Now Because:

In The Spirit Of Compassion, I Understand:

What Has Changed Now?

I Show Myself Kindness By:

In The Future, If A Similar Situation Was To Occur, I Will Handle It Better By:

I Applaud Myself For:

I'M ALLOWED TO MAKE
MISTAKES.
I'M ALLOWED TO MAKE
MISTAKES.
I'M ALLOWED TO MAKE
MISTAKES.
I'M ALLOWED TO MAKE
MISTAKES.
I'M ALLOWED TO MAKE
MISTAKES.

Date: Mood:

I Am Holding In: What I Am Expecting To Stop This Hurt Is:

I Thought: What Was Said That I Have Always
                                         Remembered Was:

What Actually Happened: Back Then, What Was Done/Said Made
                                         Me Feel:

I Accepted A Certain Type Of Behavior   I Hold Grudges Towards:
In The Past Because:

I Am Still Hurt By (Name The   What I Wish I Could Have Done
Person And/Or Behavior)   Differently:

_____

Because:

What I Lost Within Me: I Am Choosing To Let Go Of:

Continue To The Next Page

BACK THEN

I Forgive Myself For:

Now I Am Here For Myself By:

I Am Dealing With This Past Situation By:

I Forgive The Hurt And Where The Hurt Came From Because:

I Am Gentle With Myself With:

In Retrospect, I Am Doing Better Now Because:

In The Spirit Of Compassion, I Understand:

What Has Changed Now?

I Show Myself Kindness By:

In The Future, If A Similar Situation Was To Occur, I Will Handle It Better By:

I Applaud Myself For:

Date: Mood:

I Am Holding In: What I Am Expecting To Stop This Hurt Is:

I Thought: What Was Said That I Have Always
                                         Remembered Was:

What Actually Happened: Back Then, What Was Done/Said Made
                                         Me Feel:

I Accepted A Certain Type Of Behavior   I Hold Grudges Towards:
In The Past Because:

I Am Still Hurt By (Name The   What I Wish I Could Have Done
Person And/Or Behavior)   Differently:

_____

Because:

What I Lost Within Me: I Am Choosing To Let Go Of:

Continue To The Next Page

I Forgive Myself For:

Now I Am Here For Myself By:

I Am Dealing With This Past Situation By:

I Forgive The Hurt And Where The Hurt Came From Because:

I Am Gentle With Myself With:

In Retrospect, I Am Doing Better Now Because:

In The Spirit Of Compassion, I Understand:

What Has Changed Now?

I Show Myself Kindness By:

In The Future, If A Similar Situation Was To Occur, I Will Handle It Better By:

I Applaud Myself For:

Date: Mood:

I Am Holding In: What I Am Expecting To Stop This Hurt Is:

I Thought: What Was Said That I Have Always
                                           Remembered Was:

What Actually Happened: Back Then, What Was Done/Said Made
                                           Me Feel:

I Accepted A Certain Type Of Behavior   I Hold Grudges Towards:
In The Past Because:

I Am Still Hurt By (Name The   What I Wish I Could Have Done
Person And/Or Behavior)   Differently:

_____

Because:

What I Lost Within Me: I Am Choosing To Let Go Of:

Continue To The Next Page

I Forgive Myself For:

Now I Am Here For Myself By:

I Am Dealing With This Past Situation By:

I Forgive The Hurt And Where The Hurt Came From Because:

I Am Gentle With Myself With:

In Retrospect, I Am Doing Better Now Because:

In The Spirit Of Compassion, I Understand:

What Has Changed Now?

I Show Myself Kindness By:

In The Future, If A Similar Situation Was To Occur, I Will Handle It Better By:

I Applaud Myself For:

Date: Mood:

I Am Holding In: What I Am Expecting To Stop This Hurt Is:

I Thought: What Was Said That I Have Always
                                         Remembered Was:

What Actually Happened: Back Then, What Was Done/Said Made
                                         Me Feel:

I Accepted A Certain Type Of Behavior   I Hold Grudges Towards:
In The Past Because:

I Am Still Hurt By (Name The   What I Wish I Could Have Done
Person And/Or Behavior)   Differently:

_____

Because:

What I Lost Within Me: I Am Choosing To Let Go Of:

Continue To The Next Page

I Forgive Myself For:

Now I Am Here For Myself By:

I Am Dealing With This Past Situation By:

I Forgive The Hurt And Where The Hurt Came From Because:

I Am Gentle With Myself With:

In Retrospect, I Am Doing Better Now Because:

In The Spirit Of Compassion, I Understand:

What Has Changed Now?

I Show Myself Kindness By:

In The Future, If A Similar Situation Was To Occur, I Will Handle It Better By:

I Applaud Myself For:

I WILL NO LONGER JUDGE ....

BACK THEN

Date: Mood:

I Am Holding In: What I Am Expecting To Stop This Hurt Is:

I Thought: What Was Said That I Have Always Remembered Was:

What Actually Happened: Back Then, What Was Done/Said Made Me Feel:

I Accepted A Certain Type Of Behavior In The Past Because: I Hold Grudges Towards:

I Am Still Hurt By (Name The Person And/Or Behavior)   What I Wish I Could Have Done Differently:

_____

Because:

What I Lost Within Me: I Am Choosing To Let Go Of:

Continue To The Next Page

I Forgive Myself For:

Now I Am Here For Myself By:

I Am Dealing With This Past Situation By:

I Forgive The Hurt And Where The Hurt Came From Because:

I Am Gentle With Myself With:

In Retrospect, I Am Doing Better Now Because:

In The Spirit Of Compassion, I Understand:

What Has Changed Now?

I Show Myself Kindness By:

In The Future, If A Similar Situation Was To Occur, I Will Handle It Better By:

I Applaud Myself For:

Date: Mood:

I Am Holding In: What I Am Expecting To Stop This Hurt Is:

I Thought: What Was Said That I Have Always
                                   Remembered Was:

What Actually Happened: Back Then, What Was Done/Said Made
                                   Me Feel:

I Accepted A Certain Type Of Behavior   I Hold Grudges Towards:
In The Past Because:

I Am Still Hurt By (Name The   What I Wish I Could Have Done
Person And/Or Behavior)   Differently:

_____

Because:

What I Lost Within Me: I Am Choosing To Let Go Of:

Continue To The Next Page

I Forgive Myself For:

Now I Am Here For Myself By:

I Am Dealing With This Past Situation By:

I Forgive The Hurt And Where The Hurt Came From Because:

I Am Gentle With Myself With:

In Retrospect, I Am Doing Better Now Because:

In The Spirit Of Compassion, I Understand:

What Has Changed Now?

I Show Myself Kindness By:

In The Future, If A Similar Situation Was To Occur, I Will Handle It Better By:

I Applaud Myself For:

BACK THEN

Date: Mood:

I Am Holding In: What I Am Expecting To Stop This Hurt Is:

I Thought: What Was Said That I Have Always
                                    Remembered Was:

What Actually Happened: Back Then, What Was Done/Said Made
                                    Me Feel:

I Accepted A Certain Type Of Behavior   I Hold Grudges Towards:
In The Past Because:

I Am Still Hurt By (Name The   What I Wish I Could Have Done
Person And/Or Behavior)   Differently:

_____

Because:

What I Lost Within Me: I Am Choosing To Let Go Of:

Continue To The Next Page

I Forgive Myself For:

Now I Am Here For Myself By:

I Am Dealing With This Past Situation By:

I Forgive The Hurt And Where The Hurt Came From Because:

I Am Gentle With Myself With:

In Retrospect, I Am Doing Better Now Because:

In The Spirit Of Compassion, I Understand:

What Has Changed Now?

I Show Myself Kindness By:

In The Future, If A Similar Situation Was To Occur, I Will Handle It Better By:

I Applaud Myself For:

BACK THEN

Date: Mood:

I Am Holding In: What I Am Expecting To Stop This Hurt Is:

I Thought: What Was Said That I Have Always
                                         Remembered Was:

What Actually Happened: Back Then, What Was Done/Said Made
                                         Me Feel:

I Accepted A Certain Type Of Behavior   I Hold Grudges Towards:
In The Past Because:

I Am Still Hurt By (Name The   What I Wish I Could Have Done
Person And/Or Behavior)   Differently:

_____

Because:

What I Lost Within Me: I Am Choosing To Let Go Of:

Continue To The Next Page

I Forgive Myself For:

Now I Am Here For Myself By:

I Am Dealing With This Past Situation By:

I Forgive The Hurt And Where The Hurt Came From Because:

I Am Gentle With Myself With:

In Retrospect, I Am Doing Better Now Because:

In The Spirit Of Compassion, I Understand:

What Has Changed Now?

I Show Myself Kindness By:

In The Future, If A Similar Situation Was To Occur, I Will Handle It Better By:

I Applaud Myself For:

I NO LONGER CRY BECAUSE I AM HURT. I NOW CRY BECAUSE I AM GRATEFUL.

I AM GRATEFUL FOR....

Date: Mood:

I Am Holding In: What I Am Expecting To Stop This Hurt Is:

I Thought: What Was Said That I Have Always
                                         Remembered Was:

What Actually Happened: Back Then, What Was Done/Said Made
                                         Me Feel:

I Accepted A Certain Type Of Behavior   I Hold Grudges Towards:
In The Past Because:

I Am Still Hurt By (Name The   What I Wish I Could Have Done
Person And/Or Behavior)   Differently:

_____

Because:

What I Lost Within Me: I Am Choosing To Let Go Of:

Continue To The Next Page

I Forgive Myself For:

Now I Am Here For Myself By:

I Am Dealing With This Past Situation By:

I Forgive The Hurt And Where The Hurt Came From Because:

I Am Gentle With Myself With:

In Retrospect, I Am Doing Better Now Because:

In The Spirit Of Compassion, I Understand:

What Has Changed Now?

I Show Myself Kindness By:

In The Future, If A Similar Situation Was To Occur, I Will Handle It Better By:

I Applaud Myself For:

Date: Mood:

I Am Holding In: What I Am Expecting To Stop This Hurt Is:

I Thought: What Was Said That I Have Always
                                        Remembered Was:

What Actually Happened: Back Then, What Was Done/Said Made
                                        Me Feel:

I Accepted A Certain Type Of Behavior   I Hold Grudges Towards:
In The Past Because:

I Am Still Hurt By (Name The   What I Wish I Could Have Done
Person And/Or Behavior)   Differently:

_____

Because:

What I Lost Within Me: I Am Choosing To Let Go Of:

Continue To The Next Page

I Forgive Myself For:

Now I Am Here For Myself By:

I Am Dealing With This Past Situation By:

I Forgive The Hurt And Where The Hurt Came From Because:

I Am Gentle With Myself With:

In Retrospect, I Am Doing Better Now Because:

In The Spirit Of Compassion, I Understand:

What Has Changed Now?

I Show Myself Kindness By:

In The Future, If A Similar Situation Was To Occur, I Will Handle It Better By:

I Applaud Myself For:

Date: Mood:

I Am Holding In: What I Am Expecting To Stop This Hurt Is:

I Thought: What Was Said That I Have Always
                                   Remembered Was:

What Actually Happened: Back Then, What Was Done/Said Made
                                   Me Feel:

I Accepted A Certain Type Of Behavior   I Hold Grudges Towards:
In The Past Because:

I Am Still Hurt By (Name The   What I Wish I Could Have Done
Person And/Or Behavior)   Differently:

_____

Because:

What I Lost Within Me: I Am Choosing To Let Go Of:

Continue To The Next Page

119

I Forgive Myself For:

Now I Am Here For Myself By:

I Am Dealing With This Past Situation By:

I Forgive The Hurt And Where The Hurt Came From Because:

I Am Gentle With Myself With:

In Retrospect, I Am Doing Better Now Because:

In The Spirit Of Compassion, I Understand:

What Has Changed Now?

I Show Myself Kindness By:

In The Future, If A Similar Situation Was To Occur, I Will Handle It Better By:

I Applaud Myself For:

Date: Mood:

I Am Holding In: What I Am Expecting To Stop This Hurt Is:

I Thought: What Was Said That I Have Always
                                       Remembered Was:

What Actually Happened: Back Then, What Was Done/Said Made
                                       Me Feel:

I Accepted A Certain Type Of Behavior I Hold Grudges Towards:
In The Past Because:

I Am Still Hurt By (Name The   What I Wish I Could Have Done
Person And/Or Behavior)   Differently:

_____

Because:

What I Lost Within Me: I Am Choosing To Let Go Of:

Continue To The Next Page

I Forgive Myself For:

Now I Am Here For Myself By:

I Am Dealing With This Past Situation By:

I Forgive The Hurt And Where The Hurt Came From Because:

I Am Gentle With Myself With:

In Retrospect, I Am Doing Better Now Because:

In The Spirit Of Compassion, I Understand:

What Has Changed Now?

I Show Myself Kindness By:

In The Future, If A Similar Situation Was To Occur, I Will Handle It Better By:

I Applaud Myself For:

Date: Mood:

I Am Holding In: What I Am Expecting To Stop This Hurt Is:

I Thought: What Was Said That I Have Always
                                        Remembered Was:

What Actually Happened: Back Then, What Was Done/Said Made
                                        Me Feel:

I Accepted A Certain Type Of Behavior   I Hold Grudges Towards:
In The Past Because:

I Am Still Hurt By (Name The   What I Wish I Could Have Done
Person And/Or Behavior)   Differently:

_____

Because:

What I Lost Within Me: I Am Choosing To Let Go Of:

Continue To The Next Page

123

I Forgive Myself For:

Now I Am Here For Myself By:

I Am Dealing With This Past Situation By:

I Forgive The Hurt And Where The Hurt Came From Because:

I Am Gentle With Myself With:

In Retrospect, I Am Doing Better Now Because:

In The Spirit Of Compassion, I Understand:

What Has Changed Now?

I Show Myself Kindness By:

In The Future, If A Similar Situation Was To Occur, I Will Handle It Better By:

I Applaud Myself For:

I AM NOW OPTIMISTIC THAT....

Date: Mood:

I Am Holding In: What I Am Expecting To Stop This Hurt Is:

I Thought: What Was Said That I Have Always Remembered Was:

What Actually Happened: Back Then, What Was Done/Said Made Me Feel:

I Accepted A Certain Type Of Behavior   I Hold Grudges Towards:
In The Past Because:

I Am Still Hurt By (Name The   What I Wish I Could Have Done
Person And/Or Behavior)   Differently:

_____

Because:

What I Lost Within Me: I Am Choosing To Let Go Of:

Continue To The Next Page

I Forgive Myself For:

Now I Am Here For Myself By:

I Am Dealing With This Past Situation By:

I Forgive The Hurt And Where The Hurt Came From Because:

I Am Gentle With Myself With:

In Retrospect, I Am Doing Better Now Because:

In The Spirit Of Compassion, I Understand:

What Has Changed Now?

I Show Myself Kindness By:

In The Future, If A Similar Situation Was To Occur, I Will Handle It Better By:

I Applaud Myself For:

Date: Mood:

I Am Holding In: What I Am Expecting To Stop This Hurt Is:

I Thought: What Was Said That I Have Always
                                             Remembered Was:

What Actually Happened: Back Then, What Was Done/Said Made
                                             Me Feel:

I Accepted A Certain Type Of Behavior   I Hold Grudges Towards:
In The Past Because:

I Am Still Hurt By (Name The   What I Wish I Could Have Done
Person And/Or Behavior)   Differently:

_____

Because:

What I Lost Within Me: I Am Choosing To Let Go Of:

Continue To The Next Page

I Forgive Myself For:

Now I Am Here For Myself By:

I Am Dealing With This Past Situation By:

I Forgive The Hurt And Where The Hurt Came From Because:

I Am Gentle With Myself With:

In Retrospect, I Am Doing Better Now Because:

In The Spirit Of Compassion, I Understand:

What Has Changed Now?

I Show Myself Kindness By:

In The Future, If A Similar Situation Was To Occur, I Will Handle It Better By:

I Applaud Myself For:

I AM CHOOSING TO FORGIVE THOSE WHO CAN'T FORGIVE ME.

I AM HOPING THAT....

Date: Mood:

I Am Holding In: What I Am Expecting To Stop This Hurt Is:

I Thought: What Was Said That I Have Always
                                         Remembered Was:

What Actually Happened: Back Then, What Was Done/Said Made
                                         Me Feel:

I Accepted A Certain Type Of Behavior   I Hold Grudges Towards:
In The Past Because:

I Am Still Hurt By (Name The   What I Wish I Could Have Done
Person And/Or Behavior)   Differently:

_____

Because:

What I Lost Within Me: I Am Choosing To Let Go Of:

Continue To The Next Page

I Forgive Myself For:

Now I Am Here For Myself By:

I Am Dealing With This Past Situation By:

I Forgive The Hurt And Where The Hurt Came From Because:

I Am Gentle With Myself With:

In Retrospect, I Am Doing Better Now Because:

In The Spirit Of Compassion, I Understand:

What Has Changed Now?

I Show Myself Kindness By:

In The Future, If A Similar Situation Was To Occur, I Will Handle It Better By:

I Applaud Myself For:

Date: Mood:

I Am Holding In: What I Am Expecting To Stop This Hurt Is:

I Thought: What Was Said That I Have Always
                                               Remembered Was:

What Actually Happened: Back Then, What Was Done/Said Made
                                               Me Feel:

I Accepted A Certain Type Of Behavior   I Hold Grudges Towards:
In The Past Because:

I Am Still Hurt By (Name The   What I Wish I Could Have Done
Person And/Or Behavior)   Differently:

_____

Because:

What I Lost Within Me: I Am Choosing To Let Go Of:

Continue To The Next Page

I Forgive Myself For:

Now I Am Here For Myself By:

I Am Dealing With This Past Situation By:

I Forgive The Hurt And Where The Hurt Came From Because:

I Am Gentle With Myself With:

In Retrospect, I Am Doing Better Now Because:

In The Spirit Of Compassion, I Understand:

What Has Changed Now?

I Show Myself Kindness By:

In The Future, If A Similar Situation Was To Occur, I Will Handle It Better By:

I Applaud Myself For:

BACK THEN

Date: Mood:

I Am Holding In: What I Am Expecting To Stop This Hurt Is:

I Thought: What Was Said That I Have Always
                                               Remembered Was:

What Actually Happened: Back Then, What Was Done/Said Made
                                               Me Feel:

I Accepted A Certain Type Of Behavior   I Hold Grudges Towards:
In The Past Because:

I Am Still Hurt By (Name The   What I Wish I Could Have Done
Person And/Or Behavior)   Differently:

_____

Because:

What I Lost Within Me: I Am Choosing To Let Go Of:

Continue To The Next Page

I Forgive Myself For:

Now I Am Here For Myself By:

I Am Dealing With This Past Situation By:

I Forgive The Hurt And Where The Hurt Came From Because:

I Am Gentle With Myself With:

In Retrospect, I Am Doing Better Now Because:

In The Spirit Of Compassion, I Understand:

What Has Changed Now?

I Show Myself Kindness By:

In The Future, If A Similar Situation Was To Occur, I Will Handle It Better By:

I Applaud Myself For:

I BELIEVE IN UNCONDITIONAL LOVE. I DESERVE UNCONDITIONAL LOVE. I WILL GET UNCONDITIONAL LOVE. I HAVE UNCONDITIONAL LOVE.

Date: Mood:

I Am Holding In: What I Am Expecting To Stop This Hurt Is:

I Thought: What Was Said That I Have Always Remembered Was:

What Actually Happened: Back Then, What Was Done/Said Made Me Feel:

I Accepted A Certain Type Of Behavior In The Past Because: I Hold Grudges Towards:

I Am Still Hurt By (Name The Person And/Or Behavior)   What I Wish I Could Have Done Differently:

_____

Because:

What I Lost Within Me: I Am Choosing To Let Go Of:

Continue To The Next Page

I Forgive Myself For:

Now I Am Here For Myself By:

I Am Dealing With This Past Situation By:

I Forgive The Hurt And Where The Hurt Came From Because:

I Am Gentle With Myself With:

In Retrospect, I Am Doing Better Now Because:

In The Spirit Of Compassion, I Understand:

What Has Changed Now?

I Show Myself Kindness By:

In The Future, If A Similar Situation Was To Occur, I Will Handle It Better By:

I Applaud Myself For:

BACK THEN

Date: Mood:

I Am Holding In: What I Am Expecting To Stop This Hurt Is:

I Thought: What Was Said That I Have Always
                                               Remembered Was:

What Actually Happened: Back Then, What Was Done/Said Made
                                               Me Feel:

I Accepted A Certain Type Of Behavior   I Hold Grudges Towards:
In The Past Because:

I Am Still Hurt By (Name The   What I Wish I Could Have Done
Person And/Or Behavior)   Differently:

_____

Because:

What I Lost Within Me: I Am Choosing To Let Go Of:

Continue To The Next Page

I Forgive Myself For:

Now I Am Here For Myself By:

I Am Dealing With This Past Situation By:

I Forgive The Hurt And Where The Hurt Came From Because:

I Am Gentle With Myself With:

In Retrospect, I Am Doing Better Now Because:

In The Spirit Of Compassion, I Understand:

What Has Changed Now?

I Show Myself Kindness By:

In The Future, If A Similar Situation Was To Occur, I Will Handle It Better By:

I Applaud Myself For:

Section Three:

EXPERIENCED DEFEAT, BUT I AM NOT DEFEATED

EXPERIENCED DEFEAT, BUT I AM NOT DEFEATED

Date: Mood:

A Sensitive Topic For Me Is: What Was Said About Me That Has Stuck
                                         With Me?

I Easily Get Upset About: It Hurts That _____ Did

I Get Upset About It Because: What I Have Attempted To Do That Has
                                         Not Worked Out:

I Suffered From: What I Am Now Doing Differently:

Ways I Have Self Sabotage Myself: Regardless If The Statement Is True Or
                                         False, Why Do I Allow Someone's Words
                                         To Affect Me?

Continue To The Next Page

What Am I Saying To Myself That Makes Everyone Else's Thoughts About Me Irrelevant?

Right Now I Will Address _____

_____ With God.

I Have Been Feeling Down About:

I May Not Get All The Answers I Am Looking For, But My Closure Will Come From:

Because:

I Don't Fail, I:

I Know I Can Change How I Feel By:

Right Now I Am Choosing To Rise From:

I Realize That While_____ Was Done To Hurt Me, I Am:

I Understand That My Current Season Will Not Dictate:

Right Now, I Let Go Of:

EXPERIENCED DEFEAT, BUT I AM NOT DEFEATED

Date: Mood:

A Sensitive Topic For Me Is: What Was Said About Me That Has Stuck With Me?

I Easily Get Upset About: It Hurts That _____ Did

I Get Upset About It Because: What I Have Attempted To Do That Has Not Worked Out:

I Suffered From: What I Am Now Doing Differently:

Ways I Have Self Sabotage Myself: Regardless If The Statement Is True Or False, Why Do I Allow Someone's Words To Affect Me?

Continue To The Next Page

EXPERIENCED DEFEAT, BUT I AM NOT DEFEATED

What Am I Saying To Myself That Makes Everyone Else's Thoughts About Me Irrelevant?

Right Now I Will Address _____

_____ With God.

I Have Been Feeling Down About:

I May Not Get All The Answers I Am Looking For, But My Closure Will Come From:

Because:

I Don't Fail, I:

I Know I Can Change How I Feel By:

Right Now I Am Choosing To Rise From:

I Realize That While_____ Was Done To Hurt Me, I Am:

I Understand That My Current Season Will Not Dictate:

Right Now, I Let Go Of:

EXPERIENCED DEFEAT, BUT I AM NOT DEFEATED

Date: Mood:

A Sensitive Topic For Me Is: What Was Said About Me That Has Stuck
                                         With Me?

I Easily Get Upset About: It Hurts That _____ Did

I Get Upset About It Because: What I Have Attempted To Do That Has
                                         Not Worked Out:

I Suffered From: What I Am Now Doing Differently:

Ways I Have Self Sabotage Myself: Regardless If The Statement Is True Or
                                         False, Why Do I Allow Someone's Words
                                         To Affect Me?

Continue To The Next Page

What Am I Saying To Myself That Makes Everyone Else's Thoughts About Me Irrelevant?

Right Now I Will Address _____

_____ With God.

I Have Been Feeling Down About:

I May Not Get All The Answers I Am Looking For, But My Closure Will Come From:

Because:

I Don't Fail, I:

I Know I Can Change How I Feel By:

Right Now I Am Choosing To Rise From:

I Realize That While_____ Was Done To Hurt Me, I Am:

I Understand That My Current Season Will Not Dictate:

Right Now, I Let Go Of:

I REALIZED THAT WHAT WAS WEIGHING ME DOWN WAS NEVER MY WEIGHT TO CARRY.

EXPERIENCED DEFEAT, BUT I AM NOT DEFEATED

Date:

Mood:

A Sensitive Topic For Me Is:

What Was Said About Me That Has Stuck With Me?

I Easily Get Upset About:

It Hurts That _____ Did

I Get Upset About It Because:

What I Have Attempted To Do That Has Not Worked Out:

I Suffered From:

What I Am Now Doing Differently:

Ways I Have Self Sabotage Myself:

Regardless If The Statement Is True Or False, Why Do I Allow Someone's Words To Affect Me?

Continue To The Next Page

What Am I Saying To Myself That Makes Everyone Else's Thoughts About Me Irrelevant?

Right Now I Will Address _____

_____ With God.

I Have Been Feeling Down About:

I May Not Get All The Answers I Am Looking For, But My Closure Will Come From:

Because:

I Don't Fail, I:

I Know I Can Change How I Feel By:

Right Now I Am Choosing To Rise From:

I Realize That While_____ Was Done To Hurt Me, I Am:

I Understand That My Current Season Will Not Dictate:

Right Now, I Let Go Of:

EXPERIENCED DEFEAT, BUT I AM NOT DEFEATED

Date: Mood:

A Sensitive Topic For Me Is: What Was Said About Me That Has Stuck
                                         With Me?

I Easily Get Upset About: It Hurts That _____ Did

I Get Upset About It Because: What I Have Attempted To Do That Has
                                         Not Worked Out:

I Suffered From: What I Am Now Doing Differently:

Ways I Have Self Sabotage Myself: Regardless If The Statement Is True Or
                                         False, Why Do I Allow Someone's Words
                                         To Affect Me?

Continue To The Next Page

What Am I Saying To Myself That Makes Everyone Else's Thoughts About Me Irrelevant?

Right Now I Will Address _____

_____ With God.

I Have Been Feeling Down About:

I May Not Get All The Answers I Am Looking For, But My Closure Will Come From:

Because:

I Don't Fail, I:

I Know I Can Change How I Feel By:

Right Now I Am Choosing To Rise From:

I Realize That While_____ Was Done To Hurt Me, I Am:

I Understand That My Current Season Will Not Dictate:

Right Now, I Let Go Of:

I FEAR....

I CAN OVERCOME ANY FEAR.

EXPERIENCED DEFEAT, BUT I AM NOT DEFEATED

Date: Mood:

A Sensitive Topic For Me Is: What Was Said About Me That Has Stuck
                                         With Me?

I Easily Get Upset About: It Hurts That _____ Did

I Get Upset About It Because: What I Have Attempted To Do That Has
                                         Not Worked Out:

I Suffered From: What I Am Now Doing Differently:

Ways I Have Self Sabotage Myself: Regardless If The Statement Is True Or
                                         False, Why Do I Allow Someone's Words
                                         To Affect Me?

Continue To The Next Page

What Am I Saying To Myself That Makes Everyone Else's Thoughts About Me Irrelevant?

Right Now I Will Address _____

_____ With God.

I Have Been Feeling Down About:

I May Not Get All The Answers I Am Looking For, But My Closure Will Come From:

Because:

I Don't Fail, I:

I Know I Can Change How I Feel By:

Right Now I Am Choosing To Rise From:

I Realize That While_____ Was Done To Hurt Me, I Am:

I Understand That My Current Season Will Not Dictate:

Right Now, I Let Go Of:

Date:

Mood:

A Sensitive Topic For Me Is:

What Was Said About Me That Has Stuck With Me?

I Easily Get Upset About:

It Hurts That _____ Did

I Get Upset About It Because:

What I Have Attempted To Do That Has Not Worked Out:

I Suffered From:

What I Am Now Doing Differently:

Ways I Have Self Sabotage Myself:

Regardless If The Statement Is True Or False, Why Do I Allow Someone's Words To Affect Me?

Continue To The Next Page

What Am I Saying To Myself That Makes Everyone Else's Thoughts About Me Irrelevant?

Right Now I Will Address _____

_____ With God.

I Have Been Feeling Down About:

I May Not Get All The Answers I Am Looking For, But My Closure Will Come From:

Because:

I Don't Fail, I:

I Know I Can Change How I Feel By:

Right Now I Am Choosing To Rise From:

I Realize That While_____ Was Done To Hurt Me, I Am:

I Understand That My Current Season Will Not Dictate:

Right Now, I Let Go Of:

EXPERIENCED DEFEAT, BUT I AM NOT DEFEATED

Date: Mood:

A Sensitive Topic For Me Is: What Was Said About Me That Has Stuck
                                         With Me?

I Easily Get Upset About: It Hurts That _____ Did

I Get Upset About It Because: What I Have Attempted To Do That Has
                                         Not Worked Out:

I Suffered From: What I Am Now Doing Differently:

Ways I Have Self Sabotage Myself: Regardless If The Statement Is True Or
                                         False, Why Do I Allow Someone's Words
                                         To Affect Me?

Continue To The Next Page

What Am I Saying To Myself That Makes Everyone Else's Thoughts About Me Irrelevant?

Right Now I Will Address _____

_____ With God.

I Have Been Feeling Down About:

I May Not Get All The Answers I Am Looking For, But My Closure Will Come From:

Because:

I Don't Fail, I:

I Know I Can Change How I Feel By:

Right Now I Am Choosing To Rise From:

I Realize That While_____ Was Done To Hurt Me, I Am:

I Understand That My Current Season Will Not Dictate:

Right Now, I Let Go Of:

I WILL NEVER GIVE UP ON MYSELF. NEVER.

OVERTHINKING. I'VE STOPPED DOING THAT.

EXPERIENCED DEFEAT, BUT I AM NOT DEFEATED

Date: Mood:

A Sensitive Topic For Me Is: What Was Said About Me That Has Stuck
                                               With Me?

I Easily Get Upset About: It Hurts That _____ Did

I Get Upset About It Because: What I Have Attempted To Do That Has
                                               Not Worked Out:

I Suffered From: What I Am Now Doing Differently:

Ways I Have Self Sabotage Myself: Regardless If The Statement Is True Or
                                               False, Why Do I Allow Someone's Words
                                               To Affect Me?

Continue To The Next Page

EXPERIENCED DEFEAT, BUT I AM NOT DEFEATED

What Am I Saying To Myself That Makes Everyone Else's Thoughts About Me Irrelevant?

Right Now I Will Address _____

_____ With God.

I Have Been Feeling Down About:

I May Not Get All The Answers I Am Looking For, But My Closure Will Come From:

Because:

I Don't Fail, I:

I Know I Can Change How I Feel By:

Right Now I Am Choosing To Rise From:

I Realize That While_____ Was Done To Hurt Me, I Am:

I Understand That My Current Season Will Not Dictate:

Right Now, I Let Go Of:

166

EXPERIENCED DEFEAT, BUT I AM NOT DEFEATED

Date: Mood:

A Sensitive Topic For Me Is: What Was Said About Me That Has Stuck
                                         With Me?

I Easily Get Upset About: It Hurts That _____ Did

I Get Upset About It Because: What I Have Attempted To Do That Has
                                         Not Worked Out:

I Suffered From: What I Am Now Doing Differently:

Ways I Have Self Sabotage Myself: Regardless If The Statement Is True Or
                                         False, Why Do I Allow Someone's Words
                                         To Affect Me?

Continue To The Next Page

What Am I Saying To Myself That Makes Everyone Else's Thoughts About Me Irrelevant?

Right Now I Will Address _____

_____ With God.

I Have Been Feeling Down About:

I May Not Get All The Answers I Am Looking For, But My Closure Will Come From:

Because:

I Don't Fail, I:

I Know I Can Change How I Feel By:

Right Now I Am Choosing To Rise From:

I Realize That While_____ Was Done To Hurt Me, I Am:

I Understand That My Current Season Will Not Dictate:

Right Now, I Let Go Of:

EXPERIENCED DEFEAT, BUT I AM NOT DEFEATED

Date: Mood:

A Sensitive Topic For Me Is: What Was Said About Me That Has Stuck
                                         With Me?

I Easily Get Upset About: It Hurts That _____ Did

I Get Upset About It Because: What I Have Attempted To Do That Has
                                         Not Worked Out:

I Suffered From: What I Am Now Doing Differently:

Ways I Have Self Sabotage Myself: Regardless If The Statement Is True Or
                                         False, Why Do I Allow Someone's Words
                                         To Affect Me?

Continue To The Next Page

169

What Am I Saying To Myself That Makes Everyone Else's Thoughts About Me Irrelevant?

Right Now I Will Address _____

_____ With God.

I Have Been Feeling Down About:

I May Not Get All The Answers I Am Looking For, But My Closure Will Come From:

Because:

I Don't Fail, I:

I Know I Can Change How I Feel By:

Right Now I Am Choosing To Rise From:

I Realize That While_____ Was Done To Hurt Me, I Am:

I Understand That My Current Season Will Not Dictate:

Right Now, I Let Go Of:

Date: Mood:

A Sensitive Topic For Me Is: What Was Said About Me That Has Stuck With Me?

I Easily Get Upset About: It Hurts That _____ Did

I Get Upset About It Because: What I Have Attempted To Do That Has Not Worked Out:

I Suffered From: What I Am Now Doing Differently:

Ways I Have Self Sabotage Myself: Regardless If The Statement Is True Or False, Why Do I Allow Someone's Words To Affect Me?

Continue To The Next Page

What Am I Saying To Myself That Makes Everyone Else's Thoughts About Me Irrelevant?

Right Now I Will Address _____

_____ With God.

I Have Been Feeling Down About:

I May Not Get All The Answers I Am Looking For, But My Closure Will Come From:

Because:

I Don't Fail, I:

I Know I Can Change How I Feel By:

Right Now I Am Choosing To Rise From:

I Realize That While_____ Was Done To Hurt Me, I Am:

I Understand That My Current Season Will Not Dictate:

Right Now, I Let Go Of:

IT'S HARD FOR ME TO FEEL LOVED BECAUSE....

Date: Mood:

A Sensitive Topic For Me Is: What Was Said About Me That Has Stuck
                                               With Me?

I Easily Get Upset About: It Hurts That _____ Did

I Get Upset About It Because....   What I Have Attempted To Do That Has
                                               Not Worked Out:

I Suffered From: What I Am Now Doing Differently:

Ways I Have Self Sabotage Myself: Regardless If The Statement Is True Or
                                               False, Why Do I Allow Someone's Words
                                               To Affect Me?

Continue To The Next Page

What Am I Saying To Myself That Makes Everyone Else's Thoughts About Me Irrelevant?

Right Now I Will Address _____

_____ With God.

I Have Been Feeling Down About:

I May Not Get All The Answers I Am Looking For, But My Closure Will Come From:

Because:

I Don't Fail, I:

I Know I Can Change How I Feel By:

Right Now I Am Choosing To Rise From:

I Realize That While_____ Was Done To Hurt Me, I Am:

I Understand That My Current Season Will Not Dictate:

Right Now, I Let Go Of:

Date: Mood:

A Sensitive Topic For Me Is: What Was Said About Me That Has Stuck
                                               With Me?

I Easily Get Upset About: It Hurts That _____ Did

I Get Upset About It Because: What I Have Attempted To Do That Has
                                               Not Worked Out:

I Suffered From: What I Am Now Doing Differently:

Ways I Have Self Sabotage Myself: Regardless If The Statement Is True Or
                                               False, Why Do I Allow Someone's Words
                                               To Affect Me?

Continue To The Next Page

What Am I Saying To Myself That Makes Everyone Else's Thoughts About Me Irrelevant?

Right Now I Will Address _____

_____ With God.

I Have Been Feeling Down About:

I May Not Get All The Answers I Am Looking For, But My Closure Will Come From:

Because:

I Don't Fail, I:

I Know I Can Change How I Feel By:

Right Now I Am Choosing To Rise From:

I Realize That While_____ Was Done To Hurt Me, I Am:

I Understand That My Current Season Will Not Dictate:

Right Now, I Let Go Of:

EXPERIENCED DEFEAT, BUT I AM NOT DEFEATED

Date:

Mood:

A Sensitive Topic For Me Is:

What Was Said About Me That Has Stuck With Me?

I Easily Get Upset About:

It Hurts That _____ Did

I Get Upset About It Because:

What I Have Attempted To Do That Has Not Worked Out:

I Suffered From:

What I Am Now Doing Differently:

Ways I Have Self Sabotage Myself:

Regardless If The Statement Is True Or False, Why Do I Allow Someone's Words To Affect Me?

Continue To The Next Page

What Am I Saying To Myself That Makes Everyone Else's Thoughts About Me Irrelevant?

Right Now I Will Address _____

_____ With God.

I Have Been Feeling Down About:

I May Not Get All The Answers I Am Looking For, But My Closure Will Come From:

Because:

I Don't Fail, I:

I Know I Can Change How I Feel By:

Right Now I Am Choosing To Rise From:

I Realize That While_____ Was Done To Hurt Me, I Am:

I Understand That My Current Season Will Not Dictate:

Right Now, I Let Go Of:

EXPERIENCED DEFEAT, BUT I AM NOT DEFEATED

Date: Mood:

A Sensitive Topic For Me Is: What Was Said About Me That Has Stuck
                                               With Me?

I Easily Get Upset About: It Hurts That _____ Did

I Get Upset About It Because: What I Have Attempted To Do That Has
                                               Not Worked Out:

I Suffered From: What I Am Now Doing Differently:

Ways I Have Self Sabotage Myself: Regardless If The Statement Is True Or
                                               False, Why Do I Allow Someone's Words
                                               To Affect Me?

Continue To The Next Page

What Am I Saying To Myself That Makes Everyone Else's Thoughts About Me Irrelevant?

Right Now I Will Address _____

_____ With God.

I Have Been Feeling Down About:

I May Not Get All The Answers I Am Looking For, But My Closure Will Come From:

Because:

I Don't Fail, I:

I Know I Can Change How I Feel By:

Right Now I Am Choosing To Rise From:

I Realize That While_____ Was Done To Hurt Me, I Am:

I Understand That My Current Season Will Not Dictate:

Right Now, I Let Go Of:

MY ASSIGNMENT IS GREATER THAN THE THOUGHTS THAT WASTE MY TIME.

I AM CLOSER TO WHO I WANT TO BE. I AM ON THE RIGHT PATH.

Date:

Mood:

A Sensitive Topic For Me Is:

What Was Said About Me That Has Stuck With Me?

I Easily Get Upset About:

It Hurts That _____ Did

I Get Upset About It Because:

What I Have Attempted To Do That Has Not Worked Out:

I Suffered From:

What I Am Now Doing Differently:

Ways I Have Self Sabotage Myself:

Regardless If The Statement Is True Or False, Why Do I Allow Someone's Words To Affect Me?

Continue To The Next Page

What Am I Saying To Myself That Makes Everyone Else's Thoughts About Me Irrelevant?

Right Now I Will Address _____

_____ With God.

I Have Been Feeling Down About:

I May Not Get All The Answers I Am Looking For, But My Closure Will Come From:

Because:

I Don't Fail, I:

I Know I Can Change How I Feel By:

Right Now I Am Choosing To Rise From:

I Realize That While_____
Was Done To Hurt Me, I Am:

I Understand That My Current Season Will Not Dictate:

Right Now, I Let Go Of:

I AM NOT AFRAID OF ME. I WILL ALWAYS TRY AGAIN.

THE BEST WAY FOR ME TO GET RID OF UNWANTED BAGGAGE IS BY....

EXPERIENCED DEFEAT, BUT I AM NOT DEFEATED

Date: Mood:

A Sensitive Topic For Me Is: What Was Said About Me That Has Stuck
                                         With Me?

I Easily Get Upset About: It Hurts That _____ Did

I Get Upset About It Because: What I Have Attempted To Do That Has
                                         Not Worked Out:

I Suffered From: What I Am Now Doing Differently:

Ways I Have Self Sabotage Myself: Regardless If The Statement Is True Or
                                         False, Why Do I Allow Someone's Words
                                         To Affect Me?

Continue To The Next Page

What Am I Saying To Myself That Makes Everyone Else's Thoughts About Me Irrelevant?

Right Now I Will Address _____

_____ With God.

I Have Been Feeling Down About:

I May Not Get All The Answers I Am Looking For, But My Closure Will Come From:

Because:

I Don't Fail, I:

I Know I Can Change How I Feel By:

Right Now I Am Choosing To Rise From:

I Realize That While_____ Was Done To Hurt Me, I Am:

I Understand That My Current Season Will Not Dictate:

Right Now, I Let Go Of:

Date: Mood:

A Sensitive Topic For Me Is: What Was Said About Me That Has Stuck
                                         With Me?

I Easily Get Upset About: It Hurts That _____ Did

I Get Upset About It Because: What I Have Attempted To Do That Has
                                         Not Worked Out:

I Suffered From: What I Am Now Doing Differently:

Ways I Have Self Sabotage Myself: Regardless If The Statement Is True Or
                                         False, Why Do I Allow Someone's Words
                                         To Affect Me?

Continue To The Next Page

What Am I Saying To Myself That Makes Everyone Else's Thoughts About Me Irrelevant?

Right Now I Will Address _____

_____ With God.

I Have Been Feeling Down About:

I May Not Get All The Answers I Am Looking For, But My Closure Will Come From:

Because:

I Don't Fail, I:

I Know I Can Change How I Feel By:

Right Now I Am Choosing To Rise From:

I Realize That While_____ Was Done To Hurt Me, I Am:

I Understand That My Current Season Will Not Dictate:

Right Now, I Let Go Of:

EXPERIENCED DEFEAT, BUT I AM NOT DEFEATED

Date: Mood:

A Sensitive Topic For Me Is: What Was Said About Me That Has Stuck
                                                With Me?

I Easily Get Upset About: It Hurts That _____ Did

I Get Upset About It Because: What I Have Attempted To Do That Has
                                                Not Worked Out:

I Suffered From: What I Am Now Doing Differently:

Ways I Have Self Sabotage Myself: Regardless If The Statement Is True Or
                                                False, Why Do I Allow Someone's Words
                                                To Affect Me?

Continue To The Next Page

What Am I Saying To Myself That Makes Everyone Else's Thoughts About Me Irrelevant?

Right Now I Will Address _____

_____ With God.

I Have Been Feeling Down About:

I May Not Get All The Answers I Am Looking For, But My Closure Will Come From:

Because:

I Don't Fail, I:

I Know I Can Change How I Feel By:

Right Now I Am Choosing To Rise From:

I Realize That While_____ Was Done To Hurt Me, I Am:

I Understand That My Current Season Will Not Dictate:

Right Now, I Let Go Of:

I AM AWARE THAT....

INNER PEACE IS SUCCESS.

EXPERIENCED DEFEAT, BUT I AM NOT DEFEATED

Date: Mood:

A Sensitive Topic For Me Is: What Was Said About Me That Has Stuck
                                         With Me?

I Easily Get Upset About: It Hurts That _____ Did

I Get Upset About It Because: What I Have Attempted To Do That Has
                                         Not Worked Out:

I Suffered From: What I Am Now Doing Differently:

Ways I Have Self Sabotage Myself: Regardless If The Statement Is True Or
                                         False, Why Do I Allow Someone's Words
                                         To Affect Me?

Continue To The Next Page

What Am I Saying To Myself That Makes Everyone Else's Thoughts About Me Irrelevant?

Right Now I Will Address _____

_____ With God.

I Have Been Feeling Down About:

I May Not Get All The Answers I Am Looking For, But My Closure Will Come From:

Because:

I Don't Fail, I:

I Know I Can Change How I Feel By:

Right Now I Am Choosing To Rise From:

I Realize That While_____ Was Done To Hurt Me, I Am:

I Understand That My Current Season Will Not Dictate:

Right Now, I Let Go Of:

EXPERIENCED DEFEAT, BUT I AM NOT DEFEATED

Date: Mood:

A Sensitive Topic For Me Is: What Was Said About Me That Has Stuck
                                         With Me?

I Easily Get Upset About: It Hurts That _____ Did

I Get Upset About It Because: What I Have Attempted To Do That Has
                                         Not Worked Out:

I Suffered From: What I Am Now Doing Differently:

Ways I Have Self Sabotage Myself: Regardless If The Statement Is True Or
                                         False, Why Do I Allow Someone's Words
                                         To Affect Me?

Continue To The Next Page

What Am I Saying To Myself That Makes Everyone Else's Thoughts About Me Irrelevant?

Right Now I Will Address _____

_____ With God.

I Have Been Feeling Down About:

I May Not Get All The Answers I Am Looking For, But My Closure Will Come From:

Because:

I Don't Fail, I:

I Know I Can Change How I Feel By:

Right Now I Am Choosing To Rise From:

I Realize That While_____ Was Done To Hurt Me, I Am:

I Understand That My Current Season Will Not Dictate:

Right Now, I Let Go Of:

Date: Mood:

A Sensitive Topic For Me Is: What Was Said About Me That Has Stuck
                                           With Me?

I Easily Get Upset About: It Hurts That _____ Did

I Get Upset About It Because: What I Have Attempted To Do That Has
                                           Not Worked Out:

I Suffered From: What I Am Now Doing Differently:

Ways I Have Self Sabotage Myself: Regardless If The Statement Is True Or
                                           False, Why Do I Allow Someone's Words
                                           To Affect Me?

Continue To The Next Page

What Am I Saying To Myself That Makes Everyone Else's Thoughts About Me Irrelevant?

Right Now I Will Address _____

_____ With God.

I Have Been Feeling Down About:

I May Not Get All The Answers I Am Looking For, But My Closure Will Come From:

Because:

I Don't Fail, I:

I Know I Can Change How I Feel By:

Right Now I Am Choosing To Rise From:

I Realize That While_____ Was Done To Hurt Me, I Am:

I Understand That My Current Season Will Not Dictate:

Right Now, I Let Go Of:

Date: Mood:

A Sensitive Topic For Me Is: What Was Said About Me That Has Stuck
                                         With Me?

I Easily Get Upset About: It Hurts That _____ Did

I Get Upset About It Because: What I Have Attempted To Do That Has
                                         Not Worked Out:

I Suffered From: What I Am Now Doing Differently:

Ways I Have Self Sabotage Myself: Regardless If The Statement Is True Or
                                         False, Why Do I Allow Someone's Words
                                         To Affect Me?

Continue To The Next Page

What Am I Saying To Myself That Makes Everyone Else's Thoughts About Me Irrelevant?

Right Now I Will Address _____

_____ With God.

I Have Been Feeling Down About:

I May Not Get All The Answers I Am Looking For, But My Closure Will Come From:

Because:

I Don't Fail, I:

I Know I Can Change How I Feel By:

Right Now I Am Choosing To Rise From:

I Realize That While_____ Was Done To Hurt Me, I Am:

I Understand That My Current Season Will Not Dictate:

Right Now, I Let Go Of:

I'M NOT FOR EVERYONE.

Date: Mood:

A Sensitive Topic For Me Is: What Was Said About Me That Has Stuck
                                         With Me?

I Easily Get Upset About: It Hurts That _____ Did

I Get Upset About It Because: What I Have Attempted To Do That Has
                                         Not Worked Out:

I Suffered From: What I Am Now Doing Differently:

Ways I Have Self Sabotage Myself: Regardless If The Statement Is True Or
                                         False, Why Do I Allow Someone's Words
                                         To Affect Me?

Continue To The Next Page

What Am I Saying To Myself That Makes Everyone Else's Thoughts About Me Irrelevant?

Right Now I Will Address _____

_____ With God.

I Have Been Feeling Down About:

I May Not Get All The Answers I Am Looking For, But My Closure Will Come From:

Because:

I Don't Fail, I:

I Know I Can Change How I Feel By:

Right Now I Am Choosing To Rise From:

I Realize That While_____ Was Done To Hurt Me, I Am:

I Understand That My Current Season Will Not Dictate:

Right Now, I Let Go Of:

EXPERIENCED DEFEAT, BUT I AM NOT DEFEATED

Date: _____ Mood: _____

A Sensitive Topic For Me Is:

What Was Said About Me That Has Stuck With Me?

I Easily Get Upset About:

It Hurts That _____ Did

I Get Upset About It Because:

What I Have Attempted To Do That Has Not Worked Out:

I Suffered From:

What I Am Now Doing Differently:

Ways I Have Self Sabotage Myself:

Regardless If The Statement Is True Or False, Why Do I Allow Someone's Words To Affect Me?

Continue To The Next Page

What Am I Saying To Myself That Makes Everyone Else's Thoughts About Me Irrelevant?

Right Now I Will Address _____

_____ With God.

I Have Been Feeling Down About:

I May Not Get All The Answers I Am Looking For, But My Closure Will Come From:

Because:

I Don't Fail, I:

I Know I Can Change How I Feel By:

Right Now I Am Choosing To Rise From:

I Realize That While_____ Was Done To Hurt Me, I Am:

I Understand That My Current Season Will Not Dictate:

Right Now, I Let Go Of:

Date: Mood:

A Sensitive Topic For Me Is: What Was Said About Me That Has Stuck
                                         With Me?

I Easily Get Upset About: It Hurts That _____ Did

I Get Upset About It Because: What I Have Attempted To Do That Has
                                         Not Worked Out:

I Suffered From: What I Am Now Doing Differently:

Ways I Have Self Sabotage Myself: Regardless If The Statement Is True Or
                                         False, Why Do I Allow Someone's Words
                                         To Affect Me?

Continue To The Next Page

What Am I Saying To Myself That Makes Everyone Else's Thoughts About Me Irrelevant?

Right Now I Will Address _____

_____ With God.

I Have Been Feeling Down About:

I May Not Get All The Answers I Am Looking For, But My Closure Will Come From:

Because:

I Don't Fail, I:

I Know I Can Change How I Feel By:

Right Now I Am Choosing To Rise From:

I Realize That While_____ Was Done To Hurt Me, I Am:

I Understand That My Current Season Will Not Dictate:

Right Now, I Let Go Of:

EXPERIENCED DEFEAT, BUT I AM NOT DEFEATED

Date: Mood:

A Sensitive Topic For Me Is: What Was Said About Me That Has Stuck
                                               With Me?

I Easily Get Upset About: It Hurts That _____ Did

I Get Upset About It Because: What I Have Attempted To Do That Has
                                               Not Worked Out:

I Suffered From: What I Am Now Doing Differently:

Ways I Have Self Sabotage Myself: Regardless If The Statement Is True Or
                                               False, Why Do I Allow Someone's Words
                                               To Affect Me?

Continue To The Next Page

What Am I Saying To Myself That Makes Everyone Else's Thoughts About Me Irrelevant?

Right Now I Will Address _____

_____ With God.

I Have Been Feeling Down About:

I May Not Get All The Answers I Am Looking For, But My Closure Will Come From:

Because:

I Don't Fail, I:

I Know I Can Change How I Feel By:

Right Now I Am Choosing To Rise From:

I Realize That While_____ Was Done To Hurt Me, I Am:

I Understand That My Current Season Will Not Dictate:

Right Now, I Let Go Of:

SHOUTOUT TO ME AND EVERYTHING I'VE GONE THROUGH. I STILL HAVE THE ABILITY TO LOVE.

Date: Mood:

A Sensitive Topic For Me Is: What Was Said About Me That Has Stuck
                                         With Me?

I Easily Get Upset About: It Hurts That _____ Did

I Get Upset About It Because: What I Have Attempted To Do That Has
                                         Not Worked Out:

I Suffered From: What I Am Now Doing Differently:

Ways I Have Self Sabotage Myself: Regardless If The Statement Is True Or
                                         False, Why Do I Allow Someone's Words
                                         To Affect Me?

Continue To The Next Page

What Am I Saying To Myself That Makes Everyone Else's Thoughts About Me Irrelevant?

Right Now I Will Address _____

_____ With God.

I Have Been Feeling Down About:

I May Not Get All The Answers I Am Looking For, But My Closure Will Come From:

Because:

I Don't Fail, I:

I Know I Can Change How I Feel By:

Right Now I Am Choosing To Rise From:

I Realize That While_____ Was Done To Hurt Me, I Am:

I Understand That My Current Season Will Not Dictate:

Right Now, I Let Go Of:

Date: Mood:

A Sensitive Topic For Me Is: What Was Said About Me That Has Stuck
                                             With Me?

I Easily Get Upset About: It Hurts That _____ Did

I Get Upset About It Because: What I Have Attempted To Do That Has
                                             Not Worked Out:

I Suffered From: What I Am Now Doing Differently:

Ways I Have Self Sabotage Myself: Regardless If The Statement Is True Or
                                             False, Why Do I Allow Someone's Words
                                             To Affect Me?

Continue To The Next Page

What Am I Saying To Myself That Makes Everyone Else's Thoughts About Me Irrelevant?

Right Now I Will Address _____

_____ With God.

I Have Been Feeling Down About:

I May Not Get All The Answers I Am Looking For, But My Closure Will Come From:

Because:

I Don't Fail, I:

I Know I Can Change How I Feel By:

Right Now I Am Choosing To Rise From:

I Realize That While_____ Was Done To Hurt Me, I Am:

I Understand That My Current Season Will Not Dictate:

Right Now, I Let Go Of:

Date:

Mood:

A Sensitive Topic For Me Is:

What Was Said About Me That Has Stuck With Me?

I Easily Get Upset About:

It Hurts That _____ Did

I Get Upset About It Because:

What I Have Attempted To Do That Has Not Worked Out:

I Suffered From:

What I Am Now Doing Differently:

Ways I Have Self Sabotage Myself:

Regardless If The Statement Is True Or False, Why Do I Allow Someone's Words To Affect Me?

Continue To The Next Page

What Am I Saying To Myself That Makes Everyone Else's Thoughts About Me Irrelevant?

Right Now I Will Address _____

_____ With God.

I Have Been Feeling Down About:

I May Not Get All The Answers I Am Looking For, But My Closure Will Come From:

Because:

I Don't Fail, I:

I Know I Can Change How I Feel By:

Right Now I Am Choosing To Rise From:

I Realize That While_____ Was Done To Hurt Me, I Am:

I Understand That My Current Season Will Not Dictate:

Right Now, I Let Go Of:

I AM DOING MY BEST.

EXPERIENCED DEFEAT, BUT I AM NOT DEFEATED

Date: _____   Mood: _____

A Sensitive Topic For Me Is: What Was Said About Me That Has Stuck With Me?

I Easily Get Upset About: It Hurts That _____ Did

I Get Upset About It Because: What I Have Attempted To Do That Has Not Worked Out:

I Suffered From: What I Am Now Doing Differently:

Ways I Have Self Sabotage Myself: Regardless If The Statement Is True Or False, Why Do I Allow Someone's Words To Affect Me?

Continue To The Next Page

What Am I Saying To Myself That Makes Everyone Else's Thoughts About Me Irrelevant?

Right Now I Will Address _____

_____ With God.

I Have Been Feeling Down About:

I May Not Get All The Answers I Am Looking For, But My Closure Will Come From:

Because:

I Don't Fail, I:

I Know I Can Change How I Feel By:

Right Now I Am Choosing To Rise From:

I Realize That While_____ Was Done To Hurt Me, I Am:

I Understand That My Current Season Will Not Dictate:

Right Now, I Let Go Of:

Section Four:

THE BREAKDOWN

Date: Mood:

I Wanted: I Have Learned That:

I Expected: I Know I Can Receive:

I Received: I Will Continue To:

It Hurts Me To Not Receive: I Will Stop Believing:

Because: I Am Worthy Of:

When I Do Not Get What I Want, I: I Feel:

I Believe I Received This Because: I Believe That I Can And I Will:

I STOPPED STRESSING OVER EVERYONE'S EXPECTATIONS OF ME. IT WAS THEN I STARTED LIVING IN MY PEACE.

Date: Mood:

I Wanted: I Have Learned That:

I Expected: I Know I Can Receive:

I Received: I Will Continue To:

It Hurts Me To Not Receive: I Will Stop Believing:

Because: I Am Worthy Of:

When I Do Not Get What I Want, I: I Feel:

I Believe I Received This Because: I Believe That I Can And I Will:

THE BREAKDOWN

Date: Mood:

I Wanted: I Have Learned That:

I Expected: I Know I Can Receive:

I Received: I Will Continue To:

It Hurts Me To Not Receive: I Will Stop Believing:

Because: I Am Worthy Of:

When I Do Not Get What I Want, I: I Feel:

I Believe I Received This Because: I Believe That I Can And I Will:

Date: Mood:

I Wanted: I Have Learned That:

I Expected: I Know I Can Receive:

I Received: I Will Continue To:

It Hurts Me To Not Receive: I Will Stop Believing:

Because: I Am Worthy Of:

When I Do Not Get What I Want, I: I Feel:

I Believe I Received This Because: I Believe That I Can And I Will:

I AM SPECIAL. I AM DIFFERENT. I AM WORTH IT.

I AM INVESTING IN ME.
EVERYDAY. IN EVERY WAY.

THE BREAKDOWN

Date: Mood:

I Wanted: I Have Learned That:

I Expected: I Know I Can Receive:

I Received: I Will Continue To:

It Hurts Me To Not Receive: I Will Stop Believing:

Because: I Am Worthy Of:

When I Do Not Get What I Want, I: I Feel:

I Believe I Received This Because: I Believe That I Can And I Will:

I HAVE HAD VERY LITTLE TOLERANCE FOR ....

THE BREAKDOWN

Date: Mood:

I Wanted: I Have Learned That:

I Expected: I Know I Can Receive:

I Received: I Will Continue To:

It Hurts Me To Not Receive: I Will Stop Believing:

Because: I Am Worthy Of:

When I Do Not Get What I Want, I: I Feel:

I Believe I Received This Because: I Believe That I Can And I Will:

THE BREAKDOWN

Date: Mood:

I Wanted: I Have Learned That:

I Expected: I Know I Can Receive:

I Received: I Will Continue To:

It Hurts Me To Not Receive: I Will Stop Believing:

Because: I Am Worthy Of:

When I Do Not Get What I Want, I: I Feel:

I Believe I Received This Because: I Believe That I Can And I Will:

I CAN BE AT PEACE KNOWING I MADE THE BEST DECISION AT THAT MOMENT.

Date: Mood:

I Wanted: I Have Learned That:

I Expected: I Know I Can Receive:

I Received: I Will Continue To:

It Hurts Me To Not Receive: I Will Stop Believing:

Because: I Am Worthy Of:

When I Do Not Get What I Want, I: I Feel:

I Believe I Received This Because: I Believe That I Can And I Will:

THE BREAKDOWN

Date: Mood:

I Wanted: I Have Learned That:

I Expected: I Know I Can Receive:

I Received: I Will Continue To:

It Hurts Me To Not Receive: I Will Stop Believing:

Because: I Am Worthy Of:

When I Do Not Get What I Want, I: I Feel:

I Believe I Received This Because: I Believe That I Can And I Will:

THE BREAKDOWN

Date: Mood:

I Wanted: I Have Learned That:

I Expected: I Know I Can Receive:

I Received: I Will Continue To:

It Hurts Me To Not Receive: I Will Stop Believing:

Because: I Am Worthy Of:

When I Do Not Get What I Want, I: I Feel:

I Believe I Received This Because: I Believe That I Can And I Will:

Date: Mood:

I Wanted: I Have Learned That:

I Expected: I Know I Can Receive:

I Received: I Will Continue To:

It Hurts Me To Not Receive: I Will Stop Believing:

Because: I Am Worthy Of:

When I Do Not Get What I Want, I: I Feel:

I Believe I Received This Because: I Believe That I Can And I Will:

WHY DO I RECYCLE PAIN?

I CHANGED MY STATE OF MIND TO CHANGE THE QUALITY OF MY LIFE.

Date: Mood:

I Wanted: I Have Learned That:

I Expected: I Know I Can Receive:

I Received: I Will Continue To:

It Hurts Me To Not Receive: I Will Stop Believing:

Because: I Am Worthy Of:

When I Do Not Get What I Want, I: I Feel:

I Believe I Received This Because: I Believe That I Can And I Will:

THE BREAKDOWN

Date: Mood:

I Wanted: I Have Learned That:

I Expected: I Know I Can Receive:

I Received: I Will Continue To:

It Hurts Me To Not Receive: I Will Stop Believing:

Because: I Am Worthy Of:

When I Do Not Get What I Want, I: I Feel:

I Believe I Received This Because: I Believe That I Can And I Will:

THE BREAKDOWN

Date: Mood:

I Wanted: I Have Learned That:

I Expected: I Know I Can Receive:

I Received: I Will Continue To:

It Hurts Me To Not Receive: I Will Stop Believing:

Because: I Am Worthy Of:

When I Do Not Get What I Want, I: I Feel:

I Believe I Received This Because: I Believe That I Can And I Will:

MY HAPPINESS CAME WHEN I LET GO OF THE HURT.

I DO NOT NEED A REASON TO BE HAPPY. I CHOOSE TO BE HAPPY. CONDITIONS DO NOT MAKE ME HAPPY. I MAKE ME HAPPY.

THE BREAKDOWN

Date: Mood:

I Wanted: I Have Learned That:

I Expected: I Know I Can Receive:

I Received: I Will Continue To:

It Hurts Me To Not Receive: I Will Stop Believing:

Because: I Am Worthy Of:

When I Do Not Get What I Want, I: I Feel:

I Believe I Received This Because: I Believe That I Can And I Will:

THE BREAKDOWN

Date:

Mood:

I Wanted:

I Have Learned That:

I Expected:

I Know I Can Receive:

I Received:

I Will Continue To:

It Hurts Me To Not Receive:

I Will Stop Believing:

Because:

I Am Worthy Of:

When I Do Not Get What I Want, I:

I Feel:

I Believe I Received This Because:

I Believe That I Can And I Will:

IT MAY NOT HAVE WORKED OUT LAST TIME, BUT I AM BLESSED TO HAVE THE OPPORTUNITY TO TRY AGAIN.

EVERYONE WILL NOT LIKE ME. I WILL BLESS THEM ANYWAYS.

THE BREAKDOWN

Date: Mood:

I Wanted: I Have Learned That:

I Expected: I Know I Can Receive:

I Received: I Will Continue To:

It Hurts Me To Not Receive: I Will Stop Believing:

Because: I Am Worthy Of:

When I Do Not Get What I Want, I: I Feel:

I Believe I Received This Because: I Believe That I Can And I Will:

251

Date: Mood:

I Wanted: I Have Learned That:

I Expected: I Know I Can Receive:

I Received: I Will Continue To:

It Hurts Me To Not Receive: I Will Stop Believing:

Because: I Am Worthy Of:

When I Do Not Get What I Want, I: I Feel:

I Believe I Received This Because: I Believe That I Can And I Will:

THE BREAKDOWN

Date: Mood:

I Wanted: I Have Learned That:

I Expected: I Know I Can Receive:

I Received: I Will Continue To:

It Hurts Me To Not Receive: I Will Stop Believing:

Because: I Am Worthy Of:

When I Do Not Get What I Want, I: I Feel:

I Believe I Received This Because: I Believe That I Can And I Will:

I USE TO THINK THAT I DESERVED THIS HURT BECAUSE ....

BUT I NOW KNOW THAT IS NOT TRUE BECAUSE ....

THE BREAKDOWN

Date: Mood:

I Wanted: I Have Learned That:

I Expected: I Know I Can Receive:

I Received: I Will Continue To:

It Hurts Me To Not Receive: I Will Stop Believing:

Because: I Am Worthy Of:

When I Do Not Get What I Want, I: I Feel:

I Believe I Received This Because: I Believe That I Can And I Will:

THE BREAKDOWN

Date:

Mood:

I Wanted:

I Have Learned That:

I Expected:

I Know I Can Receive:

I Received:

I Will Continue To:

It Hurts Me To Not Receive:

I Will Stop Believing:

Because:

I Am Worthy Of:

When I Do Not Get What I Want, I:

I Feel:

I Believe I Received This Because:

I Believe That I Can And I Will:

THE BREAKDOWN

Date: Mood:

I Wanted: I Have Learned That:

I Expected: I Know I Can Receive:

I Received: I Will Continue To:

It Hurts Me To Not Receive: I Will Stop Believing:

Because: I Am Worthy Of:

When I Do Not Get What I Want, I: I Feel:

I Believe I Received This Because: I Believe That I Can And I Will:

I LASH OUT WHEN ....

THE BREAKDOWN

Date: Mood:

I Wanted: I Have Learned That:

I Expected: I Know I Can Receive:

I Received: I Will Continue To:

It Hurts Me To Not Receive: I Will Stop Believing:

Because: I Am Worthy Of:

When I Do Not Get What I Want, I: I Feel:

I Believe I Received This Because: I Believe That I Can And I Will:

THE BREAKDOWN

Date: Mood:

I Wanted: I Have Learned That:

I Expected: I Know I Can Receive:

I Received: I Will Continue To:

It Hurts Me To Not Receive: I Will Stop Believing:

Because: I Am Worthy Of:

When I Do Not Get What I Want, I: I Feel:

I Believe I Received This Because: I Believe That I Can And I Will:

THE BREAKDOWN

Date: Mood:

I Wanted: I Have Learned That:

I Expected: I Know I Can Receive:

I Received: I Will Continue To:

It Hurts Me To Not Receive: I Will Stop Believing:

Because: I Am Worthy Of:

When I Do Not Get What I Want, I: I Feel:

I Believe I Received This Because: I Believe That I Can And I Will:

THE BREAKDOWN

Date:

Mood:

I Wanted:

I Have Learned That:

I Expected:

I Know I Can Receive:

I Received:

I Will Continue To:

It Hurts Me To Not Receive:

I Will Stop Believing:

Because:

I Am Worthy Of:

When I Do Not Get What I Want, I:

I Feel:

I Believe I Received This Because:

I Believe That I Can And I Will:

IT DOESN'T MATTER IF PEOPLE LOVE ME OR HATE ME BECAUSE NONE OF THAT HAS ANYTHING TO DO WITH ME.

I HAVE BEEN WAITING FOR ....

THE BREAKDOWN

Date: Mood:

I Wanted: I Have Learned That:

I Expected: I Know I Can Receive:

I Received: I Will Continue To:

It Hurts Me To Not Receive: I Will Stop Believing:

Because: I Am Worthy Of:

When I Do Not Get What I Want, I: I Feel:

I Believe I Received This Because: I Believe That I Can And I Will:

THE BREAKDOWN

Date:

Mood:

I Wanted:

I Have Learned That:

I Expected:

I Know I Can Receive:

I Received:

I Will Continue To:

It Hurts Me To Not Receive:

I Will Stop Believing:

Because:

I Am Worthy Of:

When I Do Not Get What I Want, I:

I Feel:

I Believe I Received This Because:

I Believe That I Can And I Will:

THE BREAKDOWN

Date: Mood:

I Wanted: I Have Learned That:

I Expected: I Know I Can Receive:

I Received: I Will Continue To:

It Hurts Me To Not Receive: I Will Stop Believing:

Because: I Am Worthy Of:

When I Do Not Get What I Want, I: I Feel:

I Believe I Received This Because: I Believe That I Can And I Will:

THE BREAKDOWN

Date:

Mood:

I Wanted:

I Have Learned That:

I Expected:

I Know I Can Receive:

I Received:

I Will Continue To:

It Hurts Me To Not Receive:

I Will Stop Believing:

Because:

I Am Worthy Of:

When I Do Not Get What I Want, I:

I Feel:

I Believe I Received This Because:

I Believe That I Can And I Will:

THE BREAKDOWN

Date: Mood:

I Wanted: I Have Learned That:

I Expected: I Know I Can Receive:

I Received: I Will Continue To:

It Hurts Me To Not Receive: I Will Stop Believing:

Because: I Am Worthy Of:

When I Do Not Get What I Want, I: I Feel:

I Believe I Received This Because: I Believe That I Can And I Will:

I CAN PREPARE TO SUCCEED IN WHAT DIDN'T WORK OUT THE LAST TIME BY....

LOVING EVERY PART OF ME.

THE BREAKDOWN

Date: Mood:

I Wanted: I Have Learned That:

I Expected: I Know I Can Receive:

I Received: I Will Continue To:

It Hurts Me To Not Receive: I Will Stop Believing:

Because: I Am Worthy Of:

When I Do Not Get What I Want, I: I Feel:

I Believe I Received This Because: I Believe That I Can And I Will: